POWER IN CHAOS

POWER IN CHAOS

OVERCOMING ADVERSITY WITH COURAGE AND HOPE

NICK DARLAND

COPYRIGHT © 2024 NICK DARLAND
All rights reserved.

POWER IN CHAOS
Overcoming Adversity with Courage and Hope

FIRST EDITION

ISBN   978-1-5445-4590-5 *Hardcover*
           978-1-5445-4589-9 *Paperback*
           978-1-5445-4591-2 *Ebook*
           978-1-5445-4592-9 *Audiobook*

CONTENTS

PREFACE 9
1. THE CONFRONTATION 13
2. JUST A DREAM 19
3. THE MONSTER WITHIN 23
4. SIBLING LIFE 29
5. MY OWN CHAOS, PART I 33
6. MY OWN CHAOS, PART II 39
7. THE VACATION FROM HELL 45
8. BACK TO WHERE IT ALL BEGAN 49
9. TO NEW BEGINNINGS 57
10. PE IS FOR LOSERS: LIFT WEIGHTS 67
11. CITIZEN TO SOLDIER 71
12. COLLEGE AND CONSTRUCTION 81
13. DO YOUR RESEARCH BEFORE YOU COMMIT 89
14. REBIRTH 97
15. THERAPY (AND HOSPITALS) SAVE LIVES 105
16. MY REASONS WHY 113
17. HOMEREVISIONS, LLC 121
18. WE ARE CARPENTERS, ASPIRING TO BE ARTISTS 129
19. THE END OF THE STORY 137
    ACKNOWLEDGMENTS 143

PREFACE

Courage and Hope
Step into something that's bigger than you.
Imagine the things you might do.
As you grow, your heart will too.
Step into something that's bigger than you.

I WROTE THIS POEM IN 2019, AMIDST WHAT I WOULD consider the darkest moment of my life, and I have carried it with me ever since. Perhaps it, along with the experiences I will share with you throughout this book, will provide you with a hope that your own power lies within your own chaos as well. I dedicate this book to anyone who is stuck inside their own chaos. I hope you find my story to be a guide as you discover your own power. My life and the events that I will share with you have taught me many lessons. The greatest of which is to *keep going*, no matter what.

"You'll be dead or in prison by the time you're eighteen." "You only joined the army because you will never amount to anything else." "You are just a people pleaser." "Why can't you be like your brother and just fly under the radar?" "Don't even think about joining the army, you'd never make it through Basic Training." These words have burdened me for years. And now, as I write them, I choose to release the weight they've placed on my shoulders. I share my story, hoping it will touch as many people as possible. And maybe the reader will find those words "familiar" in their mind. Who has not been denigrated by people they care about? "If you judge a fish by its ability to climb a tree, it will live its whole life believing it is stupid." I heard that quote a few years ago, and I must say it speaks volumes about the early version of the Nick I once was.

I have learned throughout my (short) life that people are the answer. Everything starts with you evolving into a better version of yourself. It is a moral obligation, if you crawl out of the depths of your own hell, that you reach back and you help others. Thus, *Power in Chaos* has come to light. This is my story, my strength, my vulnerability. You are not what happens to you. None of us are. We are what we do with what happens to us. The ashes of my chaos have formed a beautiful forest for me to venture into and draw from different trees of wisdom, knowledge, and faith. I'm twenty-eight years old, and this is my story so far.

Today, as I write this book, I am a business owner of two companies. I am heavily involved in leadership throughout my community, but above all else, I am a husband and a father. I have spent twelve years in the Iowa Army National Guard. During my time in the military, I have traveled to several parts of the world—from Germany to Kosovo. I've met leaders on all fronts. Both military and civilian entities have recognized me for acts of heroism. But I am no hero; I am just a regular man. My wife, Taylor, and our two daughters are the fundamental reason for who I continue to become. I am an entrepreneur, a husband, and a father. My story, and the advice within it, stems from my life experience and different measures I have taken to invest in myself to strive to be a better version of who I was before.

I have a father, a mother, and a stepdad. Please read to the end to see how the story comes out. I have five siblings: Tyler, Shelby, Kylie, Jesse, and Jo-Jo, but only Shelby and I share both a mother and a father. All of us reacted to our upbringing in our own ways. Tyler lives with his children and girlfriend; his responsibility is to be a father to his children. Shelby's journey has landed her in Missouri, where she is happily married to her wife, Tina. Kylie has pursued a marriage to a wonderful man, and they share a beautiful life with two happy and healthy kids. Jesse and Jo-Jo are both still in school and, with the ever-evolving world around them, aspiring to be the best they can be. Jesse works for my company, HomeRevisions.

CHAPTER 1

THE CONFRONTATION

AFTER MY STEPDAD HAD FLIPPED ME OVER THE recliner and kicked me downstairs to my bedroom, I found him outside my bedroom window, screwing my window shut. When he and I confronted each other, I always left—sometimes for an hour, other times for weeks; it all depended on what had occurred. When the tensions had sufficiently eased, I went straight to my bedroom, keeping my head lowered.

This time marked a departure, as I lay in bed, weeping over the wretchedness of my life. The one thing I have always held close to from that night was the voice in my head, "Stay where you are, and you will become everything that people have always expected you to be." As that was ringing in my mind, I saw a glimpse of a life without trauma. Unsure of the path's appearance or its destination, I assumed it was preferable to my current situation. I got out of bed. My stepdad was the butt of the joke, as it turned out to be a double-hung window. I picked up the ounces of pride I had left. I pulled the window open from the top and headed east.

For seven miles, I walk, and I cry—until I reach the familiar house of my old bus driver. As I walk up to his farm, he comes outside, and he has just one question: "Things not so good at home?" "Never really are," I reply. He looks me up and down. I have on a T-shirt and shorts; my shoes and legs are caked in mud from cutting through cornfields and gravel roads to ensure no one can spot me. I ask him if I can borrow his phone to make a phone call. My plan was simple: I would call my friend Natalie in Kellogg and have her come pick me up. He happily obliges, but being the good man he always is, he insists he give me a ride back home. I have just walked seven miles to his home and am not thrilled to turn around and go back. As we are nearing my mother's house, I request that he drop me off at the neighbor's house along the road, so as not to cause any sense of my returning to anyone who might be inside.

If you've ever been through a cornfield at a full tassel, then you can understand my relief when I found out I didn't have to walk back through that. By the time I had reach my bedroom window once again, my stepdad has left for his evening job. I sneak back into my room. I pack what clothes I can, and I grab the bottle of Jack Daniels from under my bed. For the last time, I crawl back out my window and eagerly await Natalie's arrival. In the meantime, I think it would only make sense to chug the bottle of Jack. What else was I to do?

After chugging the bottle, about twenty minutes pass, and I know I am headed for the moon. It's an extraordinary level of drunkenness: you can hardly talk, and what you do say, no one can understand you. The equilibrium is so far off that you don't know if you're walking forward, backward, or side to side. I begin my trek, this time heading down the highway, hoping I would run into Natalie along the road. After I am about a mile down, she pulls up, and her helping me open the car door is a relief. I can't recall any of the ride back to her house, but I knew if I was with Natalie, I was in good hands. And a better life beckoned.

* * *

It's the second day of my senior year at Twin Cedars High School, which was in the middle of a cornfield in Bussey, Iowa (population 422). My first day was a bust: I had gotten so drunk the night before that I slept in and missed the bus. Yes, I became an alcoholic at a young age. This is something I have never admitted to myself, or anyone, but this story is about reflecting on the bad decisions I made. Alcohol was my drug of choice. Looking back on that summer going into my senior year, I drank constantly. And drinking once a week wouldn't suffice in that situation. If I didn't always have a bottle of Jack on hand, I got nervous.

    I would tuck that bottle under my bed, up against the wall and buried under some old clothing, to avoid drawing suspicion from anyone who came into my room. When I drank, I drank to forget. I drank to forget until it got to where I barely knew who I was. That was the Nick I once was, an alcoholic. I would like to paint this picture for you because I don't want you to think that after I left home, everything was rainbows.

    I come from a family of addicts, and addiction and violence run deep on all fronts. When my mom was little, the authorities sent her father to prison for murder. Later on in my mother's early childhood, my grandfather caused an accident while driving under the influence of drugs and alcohol, resulting in the passenger's death. When I was four, the DEA busted him for running drug operations out of his home. I recall my dad telling me once, "Your grandfather was the type of person who if he wanted you dead, that was something people took seriously and lost sleep over." When my grandpa got out of prison, he became a better man. He dropped the drugs, but always ensured he had his whiskey before bed every night. My mother always said it best: "Grandpa was a better grandfather than he was a dad." Hearing that statement always made me sad. However, I am thankful I got to know him and became close to him as I got older.

My dad and stepdad struggled with meth addiction. (Unfortunately, my stepdad still does to this day.) My mom's little sister's addiction to heroin is the reason we got Jo-Jo. My great-aunt (for the purposes of this story we are going to call her Karen), along with many people who stem from both sides of my family, have been consumed by their own chaotic addictions. I always said no to the drugs my family abused and manufactured. And I am proud that I have stood by that. However, I was never truly exempt from the lineal curse; my drug was alcohol—that was my coping mechanism.

My parents, including my stepdad, were all broken people who came from their own upbringing inside a broken home. If there is one thing I can guarantee from brokenness, it's like a plague, designed to infect every single person who is around you. Broken people only know one thing, and that's hurt. It is as the old saying goes, "Hurt people hurt people."

On the second day of my senior year, my great-grandfather took me to school. I remember walking into the gymnasium, still intoxicated from the night before. We were having our "Welcome back to school" assembly. I was never good at school. I always got so bored and homework to me... Yeah, I would rather have stuck my hand under a tire and let the car screech over it than do my homework. My sophomore year of high school was my worst. I received so many suspensions that the principal refused to suspend me anymore, as I was missing too much school. I stole cars and broke into people's homes. I was on court-ordered probation from the time I was fourteen to eighteen.

That night, after a hangover on the first day of my senior year, I came home. My mother and I had become so disconnected that conversation between the two of us had become nonexistent. Every time one of us opened our mouths, it was automatically an argument. I was lying on the couch, my mother in the kitchen. The arguments were so frequent that neither of us really put any effort into it anymore. That night, my stepdad just wasn't in the mood. He came into the living room and told me he was sick and tired of me, and that from then on, when I was home, I had to be in my room or not in the house at all.

By the time I had reached the age of seventeen, I had grown a quiet confidence in standing up to my stepdad. Throughout my life, there wasn't much he could do to me he hadn't already done. When he and I would argue, I would make it a point to make my stand with him every single time. However, this time may have been one stand too many. As I got off the couch, as confident as ever, my stepdad came running into the living room from my parents' room, and we just screamed back and forth. Predominately speaking, anytime a screaming match happened, a physical altercation was bound to follow. Usually, I had been pretty quick on my toes when it got to that point, but this time I wasn't quick enough. My stepdad grabbed me, threw me over the recliner without hesitation, aggressively assisted me into my room, and slammed me onto my bed. I can't remember what exactly he screamed at me, but I do remember the altercation was enough to have me in tears. Shortly after he had left my room, I found my stepdad on the outside of my window screwing the bottom sash of my window shut. He made sure I couldn't leave.

CHAPTER 2

JUST A DREAM

I WAS BORN IN KNOXVILLE, IOWA. MY MOTHER (JUST turned eighteen) and father (nineteen) were both very young in 1995 when I was born. Both my mother and father came from broken homes. They chose to have children, thinking they would do it better than their parents. I mean, is that not the goal for all of us the day our firstborn comes into this world?

My parents did the best they could with what they had. It has taken many years of my adult life to fully accept that fact. But it is so much easier for us to be surrounded by the grip of our own chaos. The outcomes of your life are just what you put into them. This I have seen for myself and my own experiences. We do the best we can. We don't always do it right, but we don't always do it wrong either. It is up to us to acknowledge ourselves and our internal decision-making and thought processes. When we do that, we can reflect on our thoughts and actions in a way that is productive. By doing so, it will allow us to step out beyond those moments.

My parents were babies having babies. My parents had yet to find themselves, let alone decide to bring a child into the world (I am glad they did). We lived in a small, single-wide trailer in a town of just 250 people called Harvey, Iowa. Just north of our lot, you could hear the train engines ensuring that industries across the nation were getting their fair share of the goods they ordered. My mother and father both worked at Vermeer in Pella. It was myself and my older brother, Tyler. He and I shared a mother, but not a father. However, Tyler and his father's story is not my story to share.

I don't have many memories of our time in Harvey, but one memory I have always held onto is that my brother, Tyler, and I shared the middle bedroom of a small, run-down trailer that sat mid-lot, nestled in misery. My parents welcomed my little sister, Shelby, just two years after my arrival into the world. One prominent memory: One morning, Tyler and I decided to give my sister a good old-fashioned Harvey-style haircut while she sat quietly in her crib. To my recollection, she didn't even attempt to cry, so I will continue to carry the assumption that we did a decent job. Our bedroom was small, with blue and red walls that my dad had painted when my parents decided the trailer was our home. My brother and I shared a bunk bed, and my sister's crib was in the back corner of what was not even an eight-foot-by-eight-foot room.

I remember at age four, my parents decided our trailer was too small, so we packed up and moved to Pershing. My mother's family had owned a piece of land there since 1848. My great-grandfather built the house that I would call home from the time I was four to the time I was seventeen.

My parents' marriage didn't last. I don't remember much about their divorce. It was when my father left that the chaos unraveled. After my parents split up, my mom suddenly found herself as a single mother, barely twenty-one years old, wondering how she could carry on into a new life. My mother went to college and got her LPN (Licensed Practitioner in Nursing) degree. She worked long hours at the nursing home in Knoxville and attended night classes at Indian Hills Community College. My dad had enough on his plate; his children just didn't seem to be the important thing to him at that time.

My first story to share is a very deep and buried memory. My hope by sharing this with you is that you recognize there is strength in vulnerability. It has taken me twenty-eight years to understand that I am not what happened to me, and neither are you.

When my mom was at work, she left us with our great-aunt Karen. To say she is a character is purely an understatement, even to this day. She lived in a blue house out in the middle of the country, outside the city limits of Bussey. It was convenient for my mother as she could get Tyler and me there on her way from work to school. She had her own problems with addiction, but I can't recall a time when I ever noticed the use of drugs while my brother and I were over.

Karen had two sons: Tanner, the elder, was fourteen and Tate was thirteen. I recall being brought with my brother into Tate's bedroom to play games. These games were not the games of cars and trucks or cops and robbers. Tate would lie in bed, naked, and he would request Tyler and me to jump from his headboard onto his genital area. Only being four and five, I don't remember Tyler and me questioning the legitimacy of Tate's decision.

But the funny thing about traumatic events is that your brain goes into protection mode and blocks out these memories. This is something I dealt with growing up, but I didn't know how to cope with it. I always knew there was something wrong with what happened in the years that Karen was entrusted with Tyler and me. However, it wasn't until I was in my teenage years that I really recognized the events that happened. Trauma is a funny thing: this wave hit me like a ton of bricks. I became angry, yet I remained silent. How could I speak of this? Who would believe me? Finally, as I got older, I mustered the confidence to approach my mom, and I let her know what had happened. When I did, she told me, "It's probably just a bad dream." Well, it wasn't. It happened, and it was the first event in my life that I draw from when I think of trauma. Now at twenty-eight years old, I carry that, but I do not let it define me.

The babysitting days at Karen's house were not long lived, as my mom had met a new man. He would soon become what people always liked to refer to as the "babysitter."

CHAPTER 3

THE MONSTER WITHIN

MY MOTHER MET A MAN, AND THEY FELL IN LOVE. I remember the first day I met him. I had come home from school, and he was with my mother in the living room. All I remember feeling was, "This isn't my dad." It wasn't long after that when my stepdad moved in. My mom was attracted to the idea of becoming a nurse and providing her family with the best possible life, given her circumstances. I believe she chose to leave her children with this man, hoping that everything would work out for the best. Little did anybody know, it wasn't a man moving into the house; it was a monster that, even to this day, I can't comprehend.

Now, before I get too far into this chapter, I want to clarify that my stepdad, from time to time, did stand out because, well, he was there when my own father wasn't. I will start with a very wonderful memory I have of my stepdad that I will forever hold close to me. When I was six, my mom enrolled me in Cub Scouts. It was one of my first Cub Scout events. It was a father-and-son camping trip, and I was so excited to have my dad with me. There was just one real problem: my dad never showed up. The scoutmasters got worried—I was the only kid there with no adult present. I just remember feeling so broken; I remember crying in the outbuilding, wondering why my dad couldn't be there.

Suddenly, my stepdad pulls into the parking lot of the camping trip and steps into the role. He was my accompanying parent during that trip, and he ensured I knew he was there. My dad got too busy to come, so instead of my mom coming to get me, my stepdad felt it would be right to give me this experience. Thank you for being there for me that day. It's a moment I will always carry with me.

The ugly side of our childhood reality, my stepdad had an aggressive meth addiction when we were little. Yes, that's the course of my entire family on all sides. If it isn't drugs, it's alcohol. Everyone in my family has a predisposition to the family curse. Unfortunately, more so than not, almost everyone has chosen that path of chaos because it's the easy route. When you're drowning, it's easy to continue drowning. You have a reason why you can't be anything else but a wicked storm of self-implosion; in the moments that implode, you have a reason.

I will never forget the feelings of coming home from school and wondering if he was in a good mood or bad. When he was in a good mood, he was great. But when he was in a bad mood, look out, because the storm was coming, and we children were his dartboard. When I explain to you, I have had my naked ass whupped, I want you to realize I had the grand pleasure of picking out my willow stick to be struck with. We would always go for the thicker ones, because if it was thicker, then it wouldn't break through the air as hard. However, that was always struck down quickly, as we had to pass what was called the "swat test." When presented with a stick, he would snatch it through the air. If it didn't crack or crack loud enough, he tossed it to the side, and we had to find another switch. We didn't dare to take too many attempts at that, because if we did, then we were looking at getting an ass whupping for taking too much time.

Out of the countless beatings, one has always stuck with me. My brother, sister, and I shared a bedroom in Pershing. As I mentioned earlier, my brother and I shared a bunk bed, and my sister had her own bed just across the room. I was in the top bunk. We had all just endured an ass whupping from the belt. Everyone was in tears and wondering where Mom was or what any of us did wrong. He would come in, whip us quickly, and then leave. It was when he left that I remember the real fear would always set in, because we knew what was coming: the check-in. After receiving our "well-deserved beating," he would come back in and check to see if anyone was still hurting or crying. If you weren't crying, then you better pretend to be crying; otherwise, you would get another belt to the bare ass.

The beating I can never forget happened to my sister. After he had finished with us, he came back for another round. My brother and I knew to keep our heads buried, pretending to be on the brink of passing out. But this time, my sister wasn't convincing enough. Suddenly, like a storm, he burst into the room, saw that Shelby could show more pain, and dragged her from her bed. In that moment, I lifted my head and saw my sister getting beaten mercilessly, with him screaming, "I'll give you a reason to fucking cry, Shelby." The belt hit hard, and while Shelby's eyes were pouring with tears, mine were full of fear.

Unfortunately, we all became conditioned to this monstrosity. At such a young age, it was all we knew. With our real dad too busy being engulfed in his own chaos, we had little outlet. We had our great-grandparents, but they always said, "We don't get involved in other people's shit." The conditioning stopped that day though. After seeing what Shelby had just endured, as soon as we could, both Tyler and I confronted my mom. Looking back on it, I do believe she always knew what was happening to us, but she chose not to accept the reality out of fear of being alone.

Regardless, after Tyler and I had shared what was happening in her absence, she confronted him, and for a moment, he left. However, it came about that he would never be gone for long. Whether it was an hour, a day, or a week, my stepdad would always find his way back into our house.

I will never forget the day my uncle and I were in the backyard. My mom and stepdad had been fighting and, in that moment, I believe my mom had my uncle take me out of the house to protect me from anything that my stepdad might do. Because when they fought, it was a vicious cycle that always ended in physical altercations and no one was exempt from the fallout of the wicked path. Just as quickly, as I am escorted to the backyard, my mom screams from the house, "Gggreeegggg!" With no hesitation, Greg sprinted through the backyard up to the house. My seven-year-old legs struggled to keep up; by the time I got there, my mom was lying in the hallway, and my stepdad was speeding off in his 1997 Dodge Dakota.

The argument, as most of them did, turned into a physical altercation where my mother had been thrown to the ground and, in a moment of fight or flight, hit him in the head with whatever object was closest to her. The only thing I can remember is the days following that incident—my mom's entire elbow was black, bruised from the physical force that she endured in this moment of violence.

The fear I shared with you and being worried if my stepdad was in a good or a bad mood is surreal. Just as I sit here and write this chapter, I am unraveled with waves of emotions, goosebumps, and memories. If he was in a bad mood, we knew our task. Come home, drop our bags, and go to bed. Not a fun route for anyone who is between the ages of four and seven, but at least we were all together and we all felt safe. I can't recall if anyone ever did anything. What I do recall is anything would set him off. Anything.

My mother's inability to take on life alone is what brought this man back into her life. Just a week or two after that awful event, he was back. The beatings didn't go away; they got worse. Except this time, it wasn't just ass whuppings. They had evolved into suffocations. It's as if he was so angry that his actions had been revealed that he wanted to punish me and show me his power and there was nothing I could do to change that. He would hold me down, hold his hand over my nose and mouth until I was just on the cusp of passing out. Then, he would let go and I would inhale a large breath, in tears. Every time this happened, he'd say, "Oh, you're crying. So obviously you can breathe."

The abuse evolved. When Tyler and I were little, we were forced to fight each other. He had a few pairs of old boxing gloves, too big for either of our hands, but most certainly made the opportunity of landing multiple blows on a small child's face much easier. Tyler would whup my ass up and down the front yard regularly, while my stepdad officiated. There is one thing I recognize now that I am older. I never gave up. If I got knocked down, no matter the pain, no matter the blindness from the tears, I never stayed down. Because of that attitude, I was crowned the nickname "Rocky." Or, if it was coming from my grandfather, "Maddog." Not knowing what that meant then, I do now, after seeing all the *Rocky* movies (not counting the *Creed* movies). As I reflect on those moments of Tyler and I pounding each other's faces in the front yard of our small-town home, I now see that even at a young age, there has always been a fighter in me.

CHAPTER 4

SIBLING LIFE

GROWING UP, MY SIBLINGS AND I WERE NEVER CLOSE. We all reacted to our upbringing in our own way. Even today, I can think of fewer than a handful of times throughout the year that we communicate. I can chalk that up to the fact that we are just different people. From my end, there is no resentment or animosity, but I don't believe it's my place to speak for them about how they feel.

Shelby and I absolutely hated each other growing up. It's as if the fact that I was born was the absolute bane of her existence. Shelby was a negative person; everything was a competition. Shelby would always tell me they adopted me from Russia. It never carried much weight as a comment from someone who thought she was a cat until she was eight.

The one thing we could both come to terms with was our father and how badly we both craved his presence in our lives. We stood next to each other in a moment of calmness, every other Friday, waiting at the front door for Dad to pull into the driveway and sweep us away from the drama of our mother's home. The unfortunate reality: my mother would often tell Shelby and me that dad wasn't coming this weekend.

While writing this, I can't help wondering if his absence was why Shelby and I clung desperately for him to just see us. I don't mean in the way of coming to spend time on his court-arranged weekends. I mean, just notice us. Just realize we exist and to want us: "Dad never comes. What am I doing wrong?" If you're reading this, I want you to know it is never you. Especially as a child, don't carry the weight of your parents' disregard as the most important thing in your life. That's their problem to navigate within themselves, not yours. When Shelby and I were young, the more important factor was drugs. When my father kicked the drugs, he got an education and from that, work.

Tyler and I were better off than Shelby and me, not that we were the best of friends. The strife on my end began when it seemed like no matter what I did, Tyler would always be better than me. Better grades, better at sports, better at drawing, better at music. Tyler was an honor roll student for as long as I can remember. My teachers were lucky if I filled in the answers to my homework just before the bell rang.

Tyler and I both played many sports, but baseball came naturally to both of us. Tyler was a hell of a pitcher. Even from an early age, Tyler could throw a baseball. I played outfield, but I could smack a ball. I had hitting ability that surpassed my age. When I was in Little League, I was brought up to the older kid team. We both received many MVPs in Little League days. It makes me smile now, thinking about being back out on the old run-down diamond playing for the Tracy Cubs.

One thing we could count on was our stepdad would be at every game. The one time I remember my father showing up was for a sophomore basketball game. I remember being excited he could finally watch me play something, but it was disappointing because I absolutely sucked at basketball. Growing up, I played football, basketball, track, and baseball. I enjoyed sports; I would be lying if I told you the only reason I embraced extracurricular activities was to be away from home as much as possible. But also, I would be fibbing if I didn't say that being away from home lightened the load.

I fell in love with speaking. I did radio news broadcasting in high school, and I was damn good at it. I can't tell you what it was that drew me to it. It was another thing to keep me away from the struggles of my home life. It was the only thing throughout my high school career that I ever made it to State in. My first-ever competition was for Districts, and I remember the only reason I didn't go to the State competition that year was because I went over my allotted time. The next year, I excelled and advanced to the State competition. I didn't advance far in the competition, but looking back on it now, I realize that speaking and writing have always been a strength of mine.

Tyler was in love with music. He was a phenomenal artist and guitar player. Truly, he could be anything he wanted to be after he graduated from high school. Unfortunately, the family curse grabbed him, and he became stuck in his own chaos. But everything you do starts with you. You can decide: "Will I do this? Or will I become that?"

Kylie was never around too much. She is our stepsister (my stepdad's daughter from a previous marriage), but regardless, we shared a childhood together, so she will always be a sister to me. Kylie was always fun to have around. She was the one sibling I never fought with. Kylie was an avid softball player, so we could always connect between softball and baseball. As the years went on, Kylie's presence faded.

CHAPTER 5

MY OWN CHAOS, PART I

I CAN'T REMEMBER WHEN I BECAME UNRAVELED trying to decide right from wrong. I can say now that it felt easier to choose what was wrong, because at least by doing so, I got some type of attention, even if it was not good attention.

The first event I can muster is the summer when I turned fourteen. My dad was living in the basement of my great-grandparents' house in Oskaloosa. It would be the first time seeing my dad in a few months, as he had been busy working a new job as a chef at the Bridgeview Center. All I ever wanted was for my dad to just notice me. *Just see that I am here.* "I'm here and I don't want to go anywhere. I need you to see me because as I get older, I can't see myself or who I'm supposed to be." That's it.

I was staying with my father, and that night was an Oskaloosa block party. My dad was doing other things with friends, so I thought it would be cool to walk up to the square and see if I could make new friends. Making friends is something I am good at. As my wife puts it, I am a social butterfly, and yes, I am. I love meeting new people. I love hearing the stories of others. Where did you come from? Where are you going? There was a time in my life when anyone was better to be with than me on my own. As I have gotten older, the only thing that has changed is my questions and the depth of the conversation I wish to have with you.

I get to the square, and I immediately meet a group of people about my age. I decided it's a good idea to sneak out of my great-grandparents' house and meet up with these kids. They weren't doing anything that night but hanging out with some eighteen-year-old who had a car and could take us anywhere the road would allow us. There was a girl, and I really thought she was the coolest person I had ever met. At the school I was attending, there wasn't much selection. But what I thought was normal, I now recognize, was a display of someone who is struggling at home. Unfortunately, in my case, the saying was, "Nick's just weird." So, I was not attracting any girls.

I wouldn't say people hated me, nor did I hate anyone. I got along with everyone on a surface level, but I certainly was not the best at showing up and being a normal kid. How do you do that when you don't know what normal is supposed to look like? So, I decided sneaking out was best; I thought this was the girl of my dreams. I went back to my grandparents at the time allotted by my father, and I made sure he saw that I had obeyed his request.

My first time sneaking out couldn't have been easier for me. My great-grandparents were saints. Truly, they were the last line holding our whole family together. (They are both now gone, so I'll take this moment to introduce them, and recognize that they were amazing people.) I make a fake body with the extra sheets that every grandparent has in the guest bedroom of their home. I walk right out the front door and just think, "Damn, it shouldn't be this easy." Turns out, it wasn't. After a fun-filled night of doing nothing but just riding around in some random dude's car, everyone decides it's time for them to go home. Everyone except for me.

I want more. I say, "Let's just keep driving. Better yet, can I drive? I have my permit." Thinking about that really made me chuckle, because that's exactly how it happened, and guess what? The kid let me drive! Oh man, that was it. I was hooked. He drove us out to a gravel road and fearlessly switched seats with me. Here was the catch: I had no experience driving a car, especially on a gravel road.

I stepped into that seat with zero fear. I could feel I had this Chevy Cavalier in my control. And control it, I did not. About four minutes after I took the wheel, we both found ourselves upside down in a ditch. Oops. The real kicker here: a local bystander saw the accident and called the police. Remember when I mentioned sneaking out shouldn't be this easy? Yeah, that came back to bite me hard.

The police officer shows up. With me being a minor, the kid who owns the car tells the officer he was driving. As the officer is dealing with the "driver" of this vehicle, he requests I contact a parent to come rescue me. I would have preferred jail. I knew my father was asleep, so I decided it would be a better idea to call my great-grandmother.

"Grandma, it's Nick."

"Nick? Nick, who?"

"It's Nick, Grandma. Could you go downstairs and wake Dad up? I snuck out and was in a car accident."

"What? Nick, you didn't sneak out. You're lying in bed."

"Oh god, they're sheets, Grandma. Can you please just go get Dad?"

She checks the bed, as if I'm playing some sick joke on her at eighty years old. "Oh, you're not here! One minute, I'll go get your dad."

All I can think is, "God, just please kill me." My dad answers, and in his confusion from still being asleep, somehow, he realizes what's going on. All I can remember was he showed up, picked me up, and took me back to my mother's house. When we arrive at about 7:30 in the morning, he just drops me off and tells my mom what had happened. He says, "Nick's your problem," and leaves. That was the beginning for me, and it compounded from there. In that moment, all I could feel was my dad never cared. I was in a car accident, and instead of being worried, he decides I'm too much for him to handle. Damn.

This night was the beginning of my adrenaline needs. The idea of being so careless and having the freedom of choice of friends intrigued me. And now as I write this, I know my "drug" of choice: freedom. Sneaking out evolved into stealing cars and breaking into people's homes, because I needed to fill that desire of adrenaline. Anyone who has ever been addicted to the rush of adrenaline will tell you, "It's a drug." It really is.

The issues at home became more and more intense. I was at an age now where my stepdad knew he couldn't just beat my ass. There is strength in knowing you've become someone who makes people recognize, "If I do this, there's the potential I could be the one who gets hurt." On the flip side of that, it just made the fights that much more intense and more aggressive from both fronts: from physical choking and being locked up against a wall, to swinging at him so hard that the garage door flies open. These things really happened, and they continued to get worse. My decision to chase freedom just got me closer and closer to prison within the confines of my mother's house.

Now, by the grace of God, I have never been to jail. How? I don't know, but I can relate to people who have been locked up. Buckle up; we're going for a ride. A buddy and I got caught stealing a car. Both of us were just fifteen. Fortunately, I wasn't the one driving, but that doesn't make me innocent. The second the trooper's lights come on, my friend reacts and stomps on the gas. Now we have lights and sirens, bringing us both back to reality. The officer, in a hurry, exits his vehicle with his pistol drawn. Woah, talk about an adrenaline rush, but not one I ever wanted to experience. He demands we both get out of the vehicle, interlock our fingers, and step backward to the sound of his voice. The next thing I know, I am handcuffed in the back of his car.

The officer breathes a sigh of relief when he realizes we are just fifteen-year-olds being dumb. Our parents come and get us, and the sentence begins: They move my bedroom upstairs. Then they install a padlock on the outside of the door, and I am confined to that room for an unannounced time. My life becomes go to school, come home from school, and go straight to the bedroom. After entering, the door is to be locked behind me so I cannot escape. I have to knock on the door for them to unlock it so I can use the bathroom.

The unfortunate reality of that event is, I wasn't handed that sentence once, but twice. The second time I snuck out, I stole my mom's car to hang out with a friend. Upon my return, my stepdad caught me red-handed. "Shit," I thought. I already knew what was coming. I grabbed my mattress, took it upstairs, and began yet another sentence. There is something about being locked up and having your freedom stripped from you that makes you think in ways that no words can express.

This is when the comments from my parents really began. They labeled me as the bad kid and said that nothing I could ever do would rescue me. Everything I did put me in the hot seat. And no matter what, I never measured up. That's when my confidence began to drain, and I felt enraged.

CHAPTER 6

MY OWN CHAOS, PART II

LET'S FAST FORWARD A FEW MONTHS TO 2011. SUMMER break is beginning, and my sister and I get to spend the summer with our father, who is now living in Grinnell. Believe it or not, it was my father's idea for us to come and stay with him. Not long before the summer began, our dad took us camping, during which he asked some questions. It was as if my dad was taking a sincere interest in the chaos at our mother's house. He probably thought if we came to stay with him for a summer, everyone would recover. Shelby and I stayed with my dad, and I was just so ready for my dad to see me. As you might expect, that wasn't the case.

To elude from the absence I felt from my dad, I found myself outside a lot. I always enjoyed walking. I would have much rather enjoyed driving, but the fact that I kept having my permit or license revoked got me real acquainted with what some would call my "lamborfeeties." One day, as I was walking around the public park, I saw a guy and some kids standing around his truck. This guy's name was Lane. Little did Lane know, but he would become my first friend from Grinnell.

Lane was a quiet country kid, who, like me, struggled to connect with people in a way that didn't involve insincerity. He and I got along immediately, and it was through Lane that I met my friends in Grinnell. Lane was a couple of years older than me, but he had a truck and people I could meet, so it was the perfect combination. He and I spent almost every day that summer together. Anywhere Lane was, more than likely, Nick was with him. Lane lived in the local trailer park with his mom. He enjoyed his cowboy hats, his belt buckles, and Ariat Roper boots. He was what one would call your "modern-day cowboy." Brantley Gilbert was Lane's favorite country singer and became mine as well. So, we immediately found ourselves with a common connection.

I met Natalie through Lane. Like Lane, Natalie was a quiet person, but unlike Lane and me, she never felt the need to put up a front to gain anyone's approval. She had a straightforward approach to life, calling things as they were—no embellishments, just honesty. This trait mirrored her parents' influence on her. Natalie had a daughter at a young age, and this experience brought us even closer. Since my mom had my brother and me when she was young, there was a cosmic connection that I believed Natalie and I had shared. Despite her youth, Natalie seamlessly passed on the values her parents instilled in her to her daughter, never once concerning herself with others' opinions. I always admired that about her.

While Natalie having a daughter wasn't the sole reason for our deep bond, it did spark our friendship early on. I was immediately smitten with her little girl, who smiled and laughed at everything I did. Although I wasn't her father, it didn't matter. Natalie and I became inseparable friends, deeply caring for each other's well-being. This foundation of genuine friendship is something I'll always cherish.

While my newfound friendships were forming, Shelby and I got jobs at Grinnell College in the dining hall. Working at the Grinnell dining facility was very beneficial for a kid who was sixteen with one goal: convince any college girl who gave me thirty seconds that I was a freshman at Grinnell College. My opening line was, "I work in the dining hall because I can give back to my school and be a productive member of society." It never really worked, but I do give myself an A for effort.

It came time for summer to end and school to start. I had worked all summer to sell the idea to my father that living with him would be in everyone's best interest. I wasn't doing well at Twin Cedars, nor was I in a good spot with my mom and stepdad, so I had a lot of motivation to make this plan work. Being the salesman I have always been, I was successful in convincing my father that I was better off living with him than I was at my mother's. I began my junior year at Grinnell High School, and I was over the moon about it. Finally, a fresh start: no more being locked in a bedroom with a mattress on the floor. No more comments; I could reinvent myself.

And reinvent myself, I did not. Turns out to reinvent yourself, it takes more than just a change of scenery. Reinventing yourself takes a willingness to do more, be more, and become more—a lesson that would still take many years for me to fully grasp. Here I am, a junior at Grinnell High School, so let's make the most of it. I'm sixteen years old, and I'm the new kid who managed to get his probation transferred from Marion County to Poweshiek County. I'll say this: it doesn't paint a great picture—being visited regularly by your juvenile probation officer. And I can't even remember why I was on probation this time.

My father and I aren't getting along. Even though I'm with him daily, I'm still not being seen. My father always showed up to work early and came home late. He went from a drug addiction to a work addiction. As much as I try in the beginning to be better, I just can't hack it. I had a role to play in this because I had a choice, and I was seen in a negative way. It's what I knew best, and so I ran with that full speed ahead.

The fallout begins with my inability to make it to school because of transportation issues. Next up were the grades. Then I began sneaking out, until I was fired by the college for spending more time talking to college girls and less time collecting trays or serving up the food.

After I lost my job, my probation officer strongly suggested I do a sport. I thought that was easy enough. I had played sports my whole life, but there's a difference between Twin Cedars and Grinnell High School. I thought maybe I'll try out for the swim team. A sixteen-year-old from a town of forty people shouldn't have any business doing competitive swimming. I was horrible at swimming, but it was something to do and kept me off the radar for the time being.

One can be as well acquainted with your lamborfeeties as you want. However, when you live in the Midwest, and you must walk back and forth from home to swim practice, there's just something about cold Iowa winters I could never hack. Even to this day, I absolutely hate winter, especially the walks home. Even though it was only a fifteen-minute walk, after being drenched from swim practice and the early morning freeze of the Midwest winter, it was miserable. However, I was committed to the team. In my whole life, I had never started a sport and didn't finish the season, so that gave me determination to move forward.

There is a positive spin to my short stint on the GHS swim team: that is where I ended up meeting my best friend, Kolton. Even to this day, he is still my person. The beautiful thing about our friendship is, when he and I first met, Kolton hated me. To him, I was the kid who had to walk to practice every morning, because by the time 6:00 a.m. rolled around, my father was already at work, and I didn't have a car. I would always get as many rides home from practice as Kolton would give me.

Without Natalie, my attendance at GHS would have deteriorated even further. Most mornings, Nat would text me as she was on her way to pick me up. The mornings Natalie couldn't get me, I would consider those an "off-day." I was never worried about my dad finding out because he was always gone.

One day, my dad receives a mid-term report: I am failing multiple classes. In a fury, he made me quit swimming. However, it would be the first thing in my life I had ever given up on, and that feeling was haunting. I could barely handle it. Everything I start, I finish. When my dad took that from me, it enraged me. I now recognize he didn't take that from me; I took it from myself by underperforming academically.

CHAPTER 7

THE VACATION FROM HELL

IT WAS DURING THE CHRISTMAS BREAK OF MY JUNIOR year when things took a turn for the absolute worse. My mom thought the family should take a vacation. To this day, it is the worst vacation of my life. Being stuck in the middle of an ocean on a cruise ship with people who didn't want me there was grueling. Nor did I honestly want to be there.

We had just ported in Cozumel, and this grand idea came upon me to buy some cigarettes. I mean, why not, when in Mexico, am I right? My plan had been successful. I had secured the package. Shelby would soon rat me out. It was the only mishap I had caused the family while we were on the entire cruise. My mom took the cigarettes and insisted that my stepdad escort me back to the ship.

I supposed everyone was at the point where the best way to deal with me was not to deal with me at all. Let me tell you, that brings a sense of loneliness that if you know, you know. And if you don't, I envy you. It sucks, it's sad, and it's self-destructive. But it doesn't always have to be. As I have said before, you choose.

While I was being escorted back to the ship, my stepdad joyfully explained to me that my attendance on this family vacation was just as he thought it would be: they should never have brought me. My response was simple: "Mom's fucking the mailman." Talk about an attitude change. For the first time, he was completely speechless. In that moment, I had all the power, and I wasn't sorry about it at all. For the first time in my sixteen years of living, I was the one bringing someone down. I was the one standing on his chest with my hand covering both his mouth and nose, absolutely refusing to let go until he cried and gasped for air. Then, I would respond with a simple statement, "Oh, come on, you're crying. So obviously you can breathe." Obviously that analogy was just a feeling. I didn't stand on his chest in the middle of the porting dock.

As my family fell apart and my mom and stepdad hid away in their room, figuring out their marriage and if what Nick said was true or not, I sat on the top deck of the cruise ship and smoked a cigar. It was a wonderful cigar too. To follow that, I found myself on the mid-deck, partying with random people just getting annihilated. This was my first actual experience with alcohol. At the time, I couldn't see any other way.

As with everything else I ever tried to do, I got caught. I stumble through the hallway to my room and find half-eaten room service outside the door of the room across the hall. I choose to delight myself in my neighbor's leftover sandwich. I look up and see my stepdad standing outside the room, staring down at me. "Oh great," I thought, "here it comes." But nothing happens. The door to the room my brother and sisters and I are sharing swings open, and I gracefully wend my way to my bunk and sleep off the drunken decisions from the night.

The next day, I find my stepdad standing on the deck, just looking out into nothing, leaning over the railing. I knew immediately that the theory I had shared with him was a fact. Have you ever had that moment? You know what I mean, you have a piece of information you know is not yours to share, but you do it anyway because it's like saying, "Fuck you." It's the only thing you think can bring you victory—making that person feel like they've made you feel over and over throughout your life.

I could see in that moment that he was broken from what I told him. I learned a large lesson that day: "Hurt people hurt people." The thing that pained me the most was that by being the person to break his spirit, even just a little, I thought it would bring me a sense of pride. It didn't. I hated myself for being that person. I learned then that I am not one who could hurt someone.

That's the lesson I took from that moment, and it's something I have had to carry with me ever since. I didn't want to be the cause of his pain. Even though it was not my act that caused it, it was my way of playing messenger with a truth that was never mine to share, especially the way that I did. Yet because I held that power and used it in a way to bring him down, I thought it would bring me up. When really all it did was bring me down even lower than he could ever bring me. I say that because I chose weakness. Weakness is darkness. Do everything you can to always be a light, even if that light is only for yourself.

No one said much to anyone the rest of the trip, and we all found ourselves back where we started, in Pershing, Iowa. However, the tables would turn for me upon my arrival.

CHAPTER 8

BACK TO WHERE IT ALL BEGAN

I HAD JUST ONE MORE NIGHT IN PERSHING AT MY mom's. I decided I would hang out with some friends from back home. While we were cruising about the streets of Knoxville, we had choked down our last cigarette. "No worries," I proudly stated; I still had my ID from working for the college, and you wouldn't believe how often that thing passed for me being eighteen.

I got the occasional "I need your license" here and there, but mostly no one questioned the ID. We made our way to the liquor store in Knoxville. I pulled up to the window and requested a pack of Marlboro Reds. The gentleman did his due diligence and requested my ID. With undeniable confidence, I handed him my ID from Grinnell College. He looked it over. I attempted to waive his attention from the idea that this is sketchy. So, I say to him, "Yeah, sorry, I go to Grinnell and I'm just home for the holidays. I don't have my license, but my parents live down the road and I can grab it if absolutely needed."

The guy looks at me, and then looks at the ID as if he is second-guessing every decision he's ever made in his life. He sells me the pack of smokes and we drive off. We don't make it but one mile down the road and I receive a phone call from my father, furious that I had just bought cigarettes from a recently retired police officer. My father and I didn't talk after that event; we both were good at shutting each other out. The next day, I was kicked out of my father's house, and Shelby took my place with him. I'll never forget that day.

When I get to my dad's, he has everything that belongs to me shoved into as many cheap Walmart Great Value brand trash bags as he had underneath his kitchen sink. It was a literal trade-off: I left, and Shelby stayed. Natalie met me at my dad's while my father and stepdad loaded up the car. As soon as Nat pulls in, I just lose it. She hugs me as I'm crying and all I can say to her is, "I don't want to go back. I can't go back." She did more for me in that moment than anyone else had ever done. She just hugged me tight and let her silence be her voice. Looking back on that day, I learned one important lesson: sometimes the best thing you can say is nothing at all.

Here I am, back at my mom's amid my own chaos. I end up back at Twin Cedars for the last half of my junior year, and things just fall apart quietly from there. The comments are back, except now it's not just my mom and stepdad, it's Tyler too. The conflict is growing between my stepdad and me, and it's only a matter of time before it gets out of hand.

There is one positive thing about being back at my mom's: I joined the Iowa Army National Guard. From a young age, I knew I always wanted to join the army. I was always intrigued with old war movies and shows. I was always the kid on the playground wanting to play war or dig trenches with wood chips for my friends and me to drive our toy cars around and imagine the impossible. However, the idea never really became real to me until a classmate of mine joined the army and we had discussed his decision to enlist. I thought, "If he could it, I sure could."

It was late April when I came home from school pondering the conversation I had with this classmate. The stars aligned that day, as I walked into the house. My stepdad is lying around watching TV. I walk into the room, and as I enter, there is a GoArmy commercial: "Be all that you can be." A combination of a conversation and a commercial brings me to say, "That looks pretty cool." He replies, "Don't even bother. You'd never do it. You wouldn't even make it through Basic Training." In that moment, I had made up my mind. There was a fire inside of me that burned so deep that the next day, I had a National Guard recruiter in my counselor's office. I was ready to enlist.

My recruiter's name was Sergeant First Class Spaur. He was a tall, lengthy guy, looking like what a military member should look like: fit, clean-shaven, and with a high and tight haircut. After a few meetings with SFC Spaur, I'm beginning the process of enlisting in the military. Here's the catch. I need my mom's and dad's signatures, as I am not eighteen yet. It took absolutely zero convincing. It seemed like everyone involved, including myself, found the idea of Nick being shipped off and not our problem very attractive.

There was one problem, though: I was on probation, again. This time, I got caught drinking and driving outside of Knoxville. I didn't get an OWI, but I did get a zero tolerance, which is the same thing. I kept this information from my recruiter until I absolutely had no choice but to let him in on my secret.

It was July 26, 2012, SFC Spaur and I were on our way to MEPS (Military Entrance and Processing Station). This trip, was attempt number two at enlisting. (The first time, they disqualified me for being allergic to morphine, so I had to obtain a medical waiver.)

Man, I'll never forget the tension in that conversation. We were about twenty minutes away from the hotel (the army makes you stay at a hotel the night before you report to MEPS).

It just came out, "I'm on probation and would like to let you know before we go any further."

He says nothing. He just pulls his car into a gas station parking lot and asks, "Why?"

"Well, this time is because I got caught drinking and driving in early June. I haven't been to juvenile court yet, but that day is coming. I lost my license though."

"Well, we made it this far. How well can you lie?"

That's what he told me to do, in my security interview: lie and hope to God it works. Well, the stars aligned, and it worked.

I enlisted the next day. I was the only kid who had no family there. At seventeen and making a big life decision like that, it hits you in the chest when you look around and see parents that took time out of their day to watch their kids step into something that is greater than themselves.

After enlisting, my recruiter asks, "Well, where do you want me to take you?"

I said, "Just take me home."

Upon arriving, I can't say there was any praise from anyone. I remember a day or two after enlisting, I got into an argument with Tyler. I can't tell you what it was about, but I remember what he said.

"The only reason you joined the army is because you're never going to amount to anything."

When Tyler said those words to me, it was a flood of feelings and thoughts of the words that so many people in my life had said to me throughout my life. "You'll be dead or in prison by the time you're eighteen." "Why can't you just be like your brother and fly under the radar." "There haven't been too many times I have been proud of you." In a moment of emotional outrage, I approached Tyler and we found ourselves back in a boxing match, except this time, neither of us was wearing gloves. *No matter what I do, it'll never be enough for anyone. So, what's the point?* After that moment, I carried the burden of those words for a long time.

The fight was quick, and Tyler's girlfriend, in a frenzy, decided to vacate the house. After the fight, I attempted to talk with Tyler and apologize for my actions. However, he wanted nothing to do with me. My actions simply reinforced his opinion as to why I would never be anything, and he left to find his girlfriend.

This would be the first time I understood what it meant to be suicidal. I thought, "I know where my stepdad keeps his pistol." In the top left drawer of his underwear drawer toward the front and to the right. I pulled out his pistol and put it to my head, but I couldn't pull the trigger. I threw the gun back where I got it. In haste, I went downstairs to my room and lost myself. After a moment of losing myself, I mustered up enough confidence to pick myself back up again. My mom was just getting home from work, and I didn't want her to know that Tyler and I had just gotten done beating the brakes off each other; more so, I didn't want any alarms going off that I was in a mental pinch. So, I got back up, left my room, and faced my unfortunate situation, hoping I could do it better without anyone noticing. *I still can't, but that's okay. I think I'm going to figure it out. I've got some things to look forward to, like joining the military. Drill weekends will be cool, and I'll meet some people I can look up to.* These were the thoughts that kept me moving forward.

In the weeks before attending my first drill, I'm finding myself absent from my mom's house completely. I've devised a plan: I'm going to move out of my mom's house, live with these people downtown in Knoxville, and I am going to get my GED. It seemed foolproof. That is, until I had my juvenile court meeting with the Juvenile PO. (I can't remember her name, but she and I had become extremely acquainted over the last year or two.) She put a stop to that. The second my mom told her I wasn't at home, she told me if I don't go home, then I'll be spending my senior year in a juvenile detention center. Whoops, so much for my plan. Here I am, once again, back to where it all began.

It was August 2012. My mom told me after the court day that if I needed to come home, she would provide a roof over my head and food for my body. I would attend drills, I would do my community service, and that was it. It was another prison sentence—except this time it would be for the year, and I had little else of a choice. I didn't think going to a juvenile home would fit well with the military. So, I left my alcohol-induced friends downtown in Knoxville.

Oh, and my first drill was absolutely God awful. I didn't know what I was doing or what to wear. My recruiter picked me up and I'm wearing cowboy boots, jeans, and a shirt. I walked into the S70 (Freedom Center at Camp Dodge). I was handed a mismatched set of PT's when I realized it is a shirt and shorts.

I asked the lady, "Do you guys have shoes you hand out? What am I supposed to do with these? I'm wearing cowboy boots."

"Wear the boots. It's your only option. Next time, show up prepared."

Lady, you have no idea who I am, and the joke's on you because there won't be a next time. I walked out of S70 and never went back to drill my entire senior year.

If you've made it this far, then thank you for being on this journey with me. It's a vulnerable one for myself. Writing this and speaking with you through my words has given me a sense of different emotions, chuckles, and memories that I had pushed down so far in the vault for so long that I had almost forgotten. The chapter is named "Back to Where It All Began." But now you and I are back to where the book starts: the day I left my own chaos for good. Get ready, because the ride gets even wilder.

CHAPTER 9

TO NEW BEGINNINGS

AUGUST 23, 2012, IS THE DAY MY LIFE WOULD CHANGE forever. God sent me, in Natalie's family, a group of people who knew I needed something. None of them knew what that was in the moment, and to be honest, neither did I. However, the time that has passed has carried us all to new beginnings.

I left my mom's and was determined to be on the right path, to do what it took to rise above my chaos. That's exactly what I did, and this time, the effect was immediate. In moments of fear, you decide: "Does the old you die?" or "Does the chaos become an even greater flame that will consume you until there is nothing left of you but a vessel?" Stepping into the things you're afraid of gives you a sense of confidence you didn't otherwise know you had. It brings up another quotation: "Adversity introduces a man to himself." That had been my entire life until that point. But here's the plot twist: for the first time, I wasn't driven by getting the attention of my parents. I was driven by giving my attention to myself and the man I was supposed to be.

I told my father I had left my mom's, and that my plan was to attend Grinnell High School, live with Natalie and her family, graduate, and go to Basic Training. Immediately my father said no. He was stuck in the mentality of, "You're too much to deal with, so you need to stay with your mom." Except this time, I stood up and refused to take no for an answer. I even went as far as setting up a meeting for my dad and Traci at her work to discuss how we could make this work. It was to no avail. He wasn't having it. I did a little research that night on Nat's phone (since I didn't have one). I learned that in the State of Iowa, a school cannot deny a student an education. I continued reading on and learned about "at risk" kids and how the public school system was to accommodate these kids to ensure their success was paved in the best way. In that moment, I conducted a flawless plan: I am going to deem myself homeless and enroll myself into Grinnell High School. (I swear, I should have been an attorney).

Grinnell High School started school the week following Twin Cedars, which worked to my benefit: Once I was there, I didn't miss a day. The first day of school, I walked into the front office of the high school and requested to enroll myself. Karma (who is Kolton's mom, now known to me as Momma K) got Mrs. Durbin, who came to the front office and asked where my parents were. I simply replied, "Oh no, it's just me. I would like to enroll myself in high school. I will deem myself homeless, so I can bypass the requirement of having to have a parent's signature on my registration form." Just so I could finish what so many people never thought I would: high school.

It was the most embarrassing time of my life. I will truly never forget walking into the main office. The kids who would be in my class were present with their parents, as I stood in front of the lady and requested that I deem myself homeless. Talk about an awkward moment. Mrs. Durbin was not qualified to take on my request, as she was just the assistant principal. The next thing I knew, I was standing in front of Mr. Sceney, the principal of GHS. I repeated my request to him. To my surprise, he allowed me to sign the forms.

Here I was, beginning what would be the start of a new life, a new Nick. Finally! I would not be Nick the troublemaker anymore. Or, Nick, the dumb shit who doesn't give a fuck about anything. I could be whoever I wanted to be. I quickly realized I was going to be Nick the homeless kid. That really hit me. It was hard for me to explain to people my situation and get my classmates to understand that I was just making a better life for myself. How do you explain that to a kid? More so, how do you explain that as a kid?

Then on to Mrs. Allen's office (the guidance counselor) to get me registered for classes and request my transcripts from Twin Cedars. Mrs. Allen remembered me from my previous year's short stint at GHS, as I was the student meeting with his probation officer.

She said, "Hey, what's going on?"

I let it all out. I can't tell you why, but there was a sense of calmness and security with her in her office. She saw I was hurting and coming from a broken place. At that moment, she did what was best for me as a human being, not what was best for the school's liability concerns. Mrs. Allen had really scooped me up and invested heart and soul into me. Thank you for your kindness to me. It went so much farther than I believed you or I ever realized. From the bottom of my heart, thank you.

Turned out, being deemed homeless opens you up to free school, free breakfast, lunches, free laptop, free registration fees—things that I did not consider when I crawled out of my bedroom window. But it did not last long. My dad caught wind of what I had done, since now my sister and I were attending the same school.

My dad texted my friend Chris, "Tell Nicolas not to get too comfortable; he's going back to his mom's."

My dad had arranged a meeting with Mrs. Allen and Mr. Sceney. The meeting was called for one purpose: to send me back to where it all began. I was called out of class and into Mrs. Allen's room, where I nervously sat on the couch right outside the counselor's office. I was trembling in fear, I knew if I ended up back at my mom's, I was destined for disaster. To me, this meeting was the difference between life and death. No matter what, I needed this meeting to go in my favor.

My dad walks in, sees me, looks at Mrs. Allen, and says, "He doesn't need to be here."

Mrs. Allen replies, "The meeting is about Nick, so Nick will be attending."

We are welcomed into the conference room by Mrs. Allen and Mr. Sceney. Mr. Sceney opens up by thanking my dad for taking the time out of his day to be here. Then follows up with, "Look, what we're doing here, I don't even know if it's legal. We understand that things at his mom's are not good, but Nick is only seventeen, and he is not legally emancipated. We would really like for you to sign his enrollment form and don't worry about lunches, breakfast, laptop, or fees; it's all covered. We just want to make sure we are doing this the right way."

My father takes a moment to muster his thoughts and begins by explaining that I need to go back to my mom's. He alludes to how he could call DHS and have them deliver me back. I sat there listening to my father belittle me and having no faith in what I could be capable of if I were just given one chance. It was a breaking moment for me, and no matter how hard I tried, I couldn't hold anything in. My father asks the room a question, I can't even tell you what that question was. The next thing I knew, the room was silent, and all eyes were on me.

I could do nothing but cry. Silently. No words, no moans, just single, heavy tears rushing from my eyes to my chin. Everyone in the room stared blankly at me for what felt like an entire minute. Not a word was said by anyone. It was as if everyone in that room could, for the moment, share the heartbreak of everything in my life I had endured that brought me to that single moment. Silence so deep you could hear my teardrops as they fell from my chin and landed on my hand.

This moment was the first time my father saw me. He broke the silence. It was as if he understood the severity of my situation at my mother's.

He then looked at me and said in a low voice, "Son, I'm going to sign these papers. I will have another conversation with Traci about your living with them. Do not make me regret this."

For me, that's all I needed. You don't realize how much power there can be, especially coming from the one person you have spent your whole life begging to be seen by. I felt relieved and at peace. My plan was being enacted, and I was following through with it.

I attended classes. I never missed one day of my senior year. I even enrolled in college classes at Iowa Valley Community College. I'll never forget my Comp 1 teacher, Laura, another person brought into my life to be a light. I learned in my senior year that I'm smarter than anyone (including myself) had ever given me credit for. I would like to share with you an email Laura sent me regarding my first paper I turned in. The paper was about me and my decision to leave my mom and take on this wild ride we call life. "See what happens when you set your mind to what you want?" This quote was the posting headline I had shared on Facebook so many years ago.

> Nick, Shit. I am sorry. The stupid email server did not send my response to you on Thursday, and I was out of town yesterday. You have a fabulous paper. Absolutely excellent. You tell us Nick's story with excellent detail and emotion. You explain the relationships and the heartaches so very well and give us such hope at the end. You should be so very proud of yourself and all that you have accomplished over the past couple of months. It takes a hell of a lot to figure out your shit and try to make a better life. It's so awesome that you are doing that.
>
> For revision, it's really just reviewing your grammar. Read through the paper again and make any changes that you know need to be made. Run grammar check if that will help you. Think of it as practice for the rest of your papers. I don't take anything off for grammar and mechanics on this paper, so you have definitely earned an A. But try to go through it on your own over the weekend before you turn in your final draft. Excellent work, Nick.

This email was the first words of kindness and validation I had ever received from someone, and it gave me a sense of purpose in the decision I had made.

Now, although I had been living with the greatest family and attending school regularly, there was still one issue. I was on probation for my drinking and driving mishap and had fines to pay. So, I set out to get a job, and a job I got! I was hired at McDonald's in Grinnell. I attended school during the day and worked as much as I could every night, most weeks. I would average close to forty hours a week.

Because I had worked so much and eaten so little, when approached by an irritated customer saying he ordered a filet-o-fish without cheese and it had cheese on it, I saw an opportunity for a quick bite as a free meal. I apologized to the gentleman and got him a new sandwich. As fast as he and I could exchange sandwiches, I went to the breakroom and ate the sandwich as fast as I could to avoid being caught. Turns out, I didn't eat it fast enough. (I now reflect on that and question a rematch: my wife tells me I devour my food faster than anyone she's ever met.) Just as I'm licking my fingers clean and hiding the evidence of the box, the shift manager comes back, absolutely disgusted. Her only response is, "You've got to go. I'm pretty sure you just broke a dozen health code violations." After McDonald's, I set my sights on Hy-Vee grocery store. I would find my place of employment for much of my senior year at Hy-Vee. It wasn't a bad gig; I just hated the red shirts they made us wear. Red has never been my color; I'm a navy-blue kind of guy.

My senior year was full of opportunities that just presented themselves naturally. Kolton and I had an agriculture class together. One day, as we were sitting in class, we just agreed to hang out: drive around Grinnell and have absolutely no destination in mind. We would just drive and listen to music. It sounds so cliché, but that's how it evolved. Kolton drove us to Ahrens Park, where he pulls into the parking lot, looks at me with a straight face, and asks, "You dip?" And dip, I absolutely did.

As I've gotten older and had my family, I have kicked the old habit. But I would be lying if I said I don't think about a can of Copenhagen Wintergreen from time to time. To the person that today is my best friend, it started with just simple memories: two kids with nothing to do but drive endlessly and pay for gas with change we could scrounge up from the jar in his car.

Not only was I creating more friendships that would last a lifetime, but certain teachers left their mark on me. One of whom I would like to introduce you to is Mrs. Wolfe. Mrs. Wolfe was Kolton and I's ag class teacher, and to this day, I still make it a point to see her from time to time. I remember Mrs. Wolfe would send me notes and tell me how proud she was of me and the work that I was doing in my studies to ensure that I was on track for graduation. She made being in class fun and is a reiteration to me that being a teacher is truly the most important job in the world. Thank you, Mrs. Wolfe, for being another light in my journey along the way.

The time spent with Natalie's family really showed me a lot, especially what a family dynamic should look like. Perfection is never the goal, but there is a significant difference between a broken family and a healthy one. I learned it's never wrong to have a servant's heart. If you get to a point in your life where you can rise above your own chaos, then you have a duty to reach out and help someone else up. Thank you, Traci, for showing that to me.

I learned that no matter what, Momma is always right. Happy wife, happy life. That doing what is right versus what you want—it'll turn out, doing what is right will always become what you really wanted in the first place. Instill your children with a mindset of being a better version of themselves than even you could have imagined. Love your children and your family no matter what, even if it isn't perfect, because it never is. Thank you, John, for showing that to me.

I learned you are not your circumstances. You can pick yourself up, and you can take a step forward. Even if it's a small and minute step, it's still a step. Don't let people bully you and hold you down. It doesn't matter what you do in this world, but do it from a place of improving the lives of those around you. And be a force for good to the most important people in your life: your children. Thank you, Nat, for showing that to me.

I graduated from GHS. I saw my mother one time during my senior year after I left. It was early in my absence from my mom's house. If you think I left and just took on the world with no personal strife, then I have done a bad job of walking you through my story. It was hard, the hardest choice I could ever make at such a young age. I was full of fear, full of doubt, full of "what ifs." But in everything you do, when it involves stepping into a better version of yourself, those thoughts and those feelings will always be there. You must go through that. It's normal, so embrace it.

I know if it is something I can do, then anyone can do it. When I left my mom's, it was not as simple as changing my life. That night, Natalie picked me up and took me in my drunken stupor back to Kellogg. I was struggling. Natalie was aware of my drinking, and I know it concerned her. I remember Natalie getting on me about drinking every day. The times I ran out of money were the nights she could sigh with relief and sleep well because she knew for the night I didn't have any liquor.

I would like to paint this picture for you because I don't want you to think I left home and immediately became a better version of myself. Even after leaving home and living with Natalie, I struggled with drinking. For more than a month, even though I was in a new environment, I was going to school daily and doing what I had to do. The force of my addiction still had its grasp on me. However, one day everything changed. This would be the day I realized something very important to me.

CHAPTER 10

PE IS FOR LOSERS: LIFT WEIGHTS

WHILE LIVING WITH NATALIE AND HER FAMILY, THEY had a neighbor across the alley who was just this monster of a man. For this chapter (and because I can't remember his name), we will call him Scott. Scott was a prison guard at Newton Prison. He had converted his garage into a home workout gym. One day after school, I didn't have to work, so back to Kellogg I went. Not because anyone made me, but because I knew if I surrounded myself with people, the inevitable is bound to happen. Turns out, strength comes in forms where you think it's weakness.

I had seen Scott from time to time, but never ventured out of my way to have a conversation with him. (It was probably because his biceps were bigger than my thighs.) When I returned home, Scott was in his garage with a recently released inmate from the prison system. (We will call him Bob.) And if you can imagine Scott being a large man, then imagine Bob being twice that. For a great visualization, if you have ever seen the movie *Pain & Gain* starring Mark Wahlberg and The Rock, Scott was Mark and Bob was The Rock.

Scott had invited me to come work out with them. I think Traci had had a quiet word with him; she wanted me to find a healthier outlet than just drinking myself into oblivion. I accepted his invitation and immediately regretted it. Ha! (I think about that day from time to time, and it just makes me laugh typing this because, man, I never knew muscles could hurt that much.) Scott and Bob showed me the ropes on simple lifts. All I can remember vividly from that day was Bob going up to Scott's in-home squat rack, slapping his ungodly oversized thighs, and saying, "You need a solid foundation if you're ever going to truly get strong."

We did the workout. For three days afterward, I walked around, unable to fully extend my arms. The thought of doing so scared me as I was convinced a full extension and locking my elbows would tear every little muscle fiber I had in my biceps (and let me tell you, it wasn't much muscle fiber). But for me, working out became my new addiction. I rabbit-holed my life watching different YouTube videos about different lifts. I had one mission: "I'm going to get so fucking huge that no one will ever think to stand in front of me." That fire was enough for me to kick alcohol for most of my senior year and get my adrenaline pumping by working my muscles daily.

I had free periods at school every day. By this time, Kolton and I had become friends, so he would take me to the college, and I would use their gym facilities. I would quiz anyone at the gym who I thought I would want to look like one day and get as much input from them as I could. My fire burned with rage my entire senior year. Instead of channeling it with alcohol, I was on a mission to become the biggest dude in all of Poweshiek County. Looking back on my pictures now, I chuckle at the thought because I was still just a small, skinny dude chasing everything for all the wrong reasons.

Frank Leahy has a famous quote, "Egotism is the anesthetic that dulls the pain of stupidity." Ever since I heard that quote in my early twenties, it has stuck with me. At the time of hearing it, I wouldn't say I correlated it with my own inner being; however, as I got older, I reflected on the things I did—If you have an oversized ego, no matter who you are or what you do, you will always make a fool of yourself.

I must give myself credit, though, for the journey of weightlifting during my senior year. I was always an active kid; I played sports. In my senior year, I chose to just focus on weightlifting. When I enlisted in the army, in my junior year of high school, I remember I barely made the weight minimum: I was 140-something pounds; I had just landed on the minimum. When I graduated from GHS, I was 167 pounds. I remember that vividly, being so happy; I was gaining weight and building muscle.

Weightlifting became the light of getting out of my chaos. You must become a light for yourself. You must find a reason within you that is not fueled by rage or darkness. My senior year, I was in PE classes, and I found out that GHS offered a strength-training class. It was like PE, except you spent forty minutes in the weight room picking up ungodly amounts of weight, barely even supervised. But that was fine, because for me, it was an opportunity to indulge my newfound addiction. I requested to drop my PE class and in exchange pick up the strength-training class. I found it much more beneficial to keep progressing on my weight training rather than play pickleball with random groups in the gym. Mrs. Allen was a fan of mine by that time. She happily obliged and worked with me to make the switch.

CHAPTER 11

CITIZEN TO SOLDIER

BEFORE WE DELVE TOO FAR, I WANT TO MAKE IT known that I have spent twelve proud years in the Iowa Army National Guard. As you read this chapter, you will see that my early years were challenging, and that is on me. However, I humbly say that I grew to be an influential leader within the organization. Like every good leader, I hold the bad experiences just as closely as the good ones. You learn from both sides of the coin. The military saved my life twice, and I deeply value and cherish my service to the Iowa National Guard as an organization and all those who have invested in me along the way. Most importantly, I cherish the troops I have been able to help guide and walk with during their challenging journeys.

Let's take a walk through my early years in the military. As I stated earlier, my first drill in the Guard did not end well. Not for me, nor for them. However, little did they know that I'm Nick Darland, and I know how to hold a grudge. The entirety of my senior year, I was expected to be at drill. In Iowa we call them "RSP"—don't ask me what it stands for because I never attended them. Every month, it was like clockwork. I would get a call at around 7:20 in the morning from SFC Hughes asking if I was going to attend drill this month. "Nope," I would reply every time. Now, I can't explain why, nor did I ever ask him, but every month I would get $86.00 deposited into my account for a half-day attendance at RSP. Remember when I said that when you step out into a greater version of you, everything falls into place the way it's supposed to? Well, I mean that.

You see, my intentions were simple. Screw the military. They hurt me at my first drill and made a fool of me. I didn't care if they gave me a dishonorable discharge. Finally, it got to a point where Hughes showed up in Grinnell, and he was with another gentleman. I was very upfront with Hughes. I told him to cancel my contract.

"I changed my mind. Now that I'm graduated, I'm going to college."

He said, "I don't have that authority."

Turns out, Hughes had that authority, but he didn't want me to miss an opportunity he knew would be best for me. I was attending what we call "Blue Phase" of RSP (it has three different phases: Red, White, and Blue). The troops getting ready to ship out were meant to attend Blue Phase, and I had to be there to receive my orders.

"Don't worry," Hughes assured me, "you will be done by noon."

That meant he would let me go home. That Saturday morning, I'm sitting in a briefing room with a few other guys and Hughes walks in to give us an informational briefing about what to expect.

He says to the room, "If you get a tattoo between now and the time you ship out, I am going to discharge you."

I thought to myself, "You fucker, you told me you didn't have that authority." Ha!

Hughes refused to let me quit the military. That was the greatest decision another person could have made for me. I attended Basic Training. The year is 2013 and the date is September 13. (Anyone else in the military remember their ship date for BCT?) I will always remember that day, as it was a day of mixed emotions. I was scared; I was eager, but most importantly, I looked pretty good from the last year of working out. (Insert big ego joke here.)

I'll never forget the day I landed in Columbia, South Carolina. The drill sergeants awaited our arrival and had us form up in the middle of the airport. From there, we boarded a bus and were taken to Fort Jackson, South Carolina (otherwise known as "Relaxin' Jackson"). There wasn't much relaxing about it. Basic Training was right up my alley. I remember the shark attack. This is your first day of BCT, and the drill sergeants have an absolute heyday attempting to intimidate you. If you showed weakness, you automatically became a target.

Turns out, I was damn good at being yelled at and challenged to quit—even though I never did. My day started by being abruptly awakened by our drill sergeants. We were given no time at all to get dressed, and could only make a quick lap through the bathroom to ensure we were clean shaven. As I pressed for a spot at a sink, I gashed my chin open with my razor. My chin bled and bled; it wouldn't stop. The drill sergeants advised me to spend a day at sick call, but I respectfully refused. You see, a day at sick call meant a day lost in training. Not only that, but you spent the day on the bleachers. As training went on, more and more people would find themselves on the bleachers because of different injuries. Some legit but most not. To me, time on the bleachers meant you didn't measure up. My commitment to myself was to never find myself on the bleachers.

My bunkmate, Chen, was a good fellow who would always kick my ass during fire guard in a game called Dots and Boxes. Chen was a fabulous individual from China who joined the military to help with college and obtain citizenship. The dude was smart, and too smart for eighteen-year-old Nick to think he could ever one-up him on Dots and Boxes. Well, Chen, by the chance you ever read this, this is my official rematch callout to you!

Another great gentleman I have never forgotten is DeAngelo. He was five or so years older than me, and he had a ton of wisdom for his age. We would spend many hours together talking about various life situations. He was a man of God, which was for me something I could never latch onto. One day, when we were out on the ranges, DeAngelo and I were sitting under a shade tree, and he was reading his Bible.

I asked, "What part of the scripture are you reading?"

He responded, "Proverbs, it's my favorite book in the Bible."

I asked, "What's your favorite verse?"

"Proverbs 3: 5–6: 'Trust in the Lord with all your heart, and lean not on your own understanding. In all your ways acknowledge him, and he will direct your paths.'"

That moment rang true to me. I began carrying a little Army Bible in my left jacket pocket and reading that book every chance I could. I attended church every Sunday with DeAngelo. Finally, at the end of Basic Training, at eighteen years old, I was baptized. It was a beautiful moment. I had Proverbs 3:5–6 tattooed over my heart.

Following Basic, I attended Advanced Individual Training (AIT) at Fort Lee, Virginia. AIT was the opposite side of the coin. Basic was very intense: you didn't go to the bathroom without asking and taking someone with you. You couldn't even have Gatorade while at Basic. No phones, nothing. Then to AIT, where there was a smoke pit right outside your barracks and a convenience store just a short walk away. AIT was much more relaxed than I could have ever thought possible. I went from having a drill sergeant to having a platoon sergeant. Once you spent a couple weeks on post, they gave you passes on the weekends to go out and about and see some sights.

I have always been fascinated with history, especially if I stood at a spot where, through time, something so significant happened that people thought of recording it. I visited Petersburg, Richmond, and Civil War battlefields many times. Each time was the same destination, but a different journey.

I graduated from AIT and returned home, where I was recognized by the Iowa National Guard with the Iowa Leadership Ribbon with the Torch for my superior service. It was the first time in my life I had ever been recognized for something significant, and it was a truly humbling experience.

Upon my return home, I was brimming with ambition and a determination to surpass what I had just achieved. However, I encountered a formidable obstacle—myself. Initially, everything seemed promising, gleaming with a newfound perspective and a somewhat uncertain foundation to build upon. However, the stark reality soon set in: I had not been equipped with the essential tools for success during my upbringing.

The echoes of a victim mentality, deeply ingrained from years past, resurfaced sooner than I cared to admit. Despite my efforts to forge a new path, the familiar patterns persisted. Each time I attempted to ascend, I found myself ensnared once more by the same self-defeating mindset. The cycle of progress and regression became all too familiar, leaving me feeling as though every advancement was inevitably followed by a precipitous decline.

In my first five years of service (minus the time I was in a controlled environment), I was never a troop that was good with authority. If you didn't respect me, I sure as shit didn't respect you. That attitude found me in the grip of a lot of heat from some higher-ranking officials throughout my early career. I was never the troop that many people could rely too much on early in my career. To be honest, it stems from the most honest statement. I had a shit attitude and an even worse mentality. I couldn't seem to figure out why my life was so shitty—turns out it was me that was causing 99 percent of my own problems at that time.

I like to refer to my first enlistment as my "transformative period." By the time I was nearing my six-year commitment, I had begun to work on myself and realized that I had the control to create my reality. With that newfound mentality, I began to go from "Fuck everyone!" to "What am I doing wrong?" or "How can I implement a better mindset and maybe project that new mindset outward?"—I went from the troop who hated drill and everyone at it to the troop who wanted to reenlist because I was going to do it for me, and I was choosing to be a part of the solution rather than the problem. On July 26, 2018, I would raise my right hand and reenlist, this time, with the intention of truly being all I can be.

Although I originally enlisted with the mindset of *I'm going to prove you wrong*, I do value my first six years in the military. No matter what I did, regardless of right, wrong, or indifferent. I chose to do more, be more, and become more.

No longer part of the problem, part of the solution. Today, I see so many brand-new troops who share a beginning similar to what I had, and I can be that leader for them. I can connect with these troops and be a living example that hey, you ARE NOT what happens to you, you are not your family, and you are not your environment.

To bring that last paragraph into perspective for you and help me paint this picture. Recently, I was speaking with a junior enlisted who, at the time, was just struggling with surviving. As he was talking to me, it very quickly became a conversation of, "Troop, I know exactly what you're saying, and I want you to know there is most certainly a way out if you are committed to yourself. You have to work on you—change your mind, and you will change your life. A few months go by, and this troop calls me out of nowhere; I answer, excited to see what he's been up to, and he starts the conversation like this: "Hey Sarge, I just want you to know that I am doing really good. I took your advice, and I found a mental health counselor that I am working with every week, I got a new job, and I kicked my roommate out. I just wanted to call you and thank you for taking the time to listen to me and help guide me on a better path and mindset. I have really held your words close to me."

Jim Rohn once said, "Here's what's important to me, is for my name once in a while to appear in someone's testimonial." When I heard that at a younger age, I never thought much of it. However, as I get older and wiser, those words ring louder and louder with every conversation. And more so than not, it is the conversation(s) behind closed doors that are held private that have the greatest impact on others. Not the seminars, not the lectures, but the humanity of being a person to take a moment and just listen. It is the leader I have grown to be, not only in uniform but in my companies as well.

Furthermore, that doesn't mean that bad leaders don't exist. Bad leaders exist everywhere; to be honest, I have learned more from bad leaders than I have from good ones. Today, when I experience a brand new E5 or an overly ego-consumed 2nd LT, I take the opportunity to have what I call a "teachable moment." I don't call you out, I don't belittle you, I simply find a good time to have an open-ended conversation that encourages you to reflect on your actions. Let's work together to be better for ourselves and our troops. It is as I tell leaders in my companies, "Whether you think so or not, everyone is always watching you." So, be the person that you would want to see every single day.

Although I never got the chance to deploy, throughout my career, the army provided me with many opportunities to see the world. My first time abroad was an overseas annual training event in Germany. Finding myself in the mountain range of Hohenfels, it was truly a wonderful experience for me. I was able to experience a completely different culture at such a young age and more importantly, get paid and fed while I did it.

Another of those opportunities was traveling to Kosovo in June of 2021 on NATO orders to represent the Iowa National Guard working with the Kosovo Security Force on maintenance operations. It was a great time, and Kosovo is a beautiful country. A few other troops (Colonel, Chief Warrant Officer 5, and Master Sergeant) and I were all invited on this trip. The locals and the embassy put us up in a nice hotel and wined and dined us every day.

My military service came and went. As of July 26, 2024, I am no longer wearing the uniform. As I transition back from Soldier to Citizen, I find myself profoundly proud to have served and forever thankful to a man who wouldn't let me quit and an organization full of people from all walks of life. I fell in love with an ecosystem that so many people shy away from. Without realizing it, the army created a solid foundation for me. And my last six years have been dedicated to helping other troops get a better balance on their foundation. I would recommend joining to anyone, especially if you have absolutely no idea what you're doing—why not see who you could become or even more importantly, the people you could influence along the way? However, most importantly, as the Army would have it, "Be all you can be."

CHAPTER 12

COLLEGE AND CONSTRUCTION

IN 2014, I AM LIVING IN INDIANOLA IN MY VERY FIRST apartment. (I moved to Indianola because that is where my girlfriend at the time lived.) I have just recently returned from AIT, and I am ready to get started on the next journey: college at Des Moines Area Community College (DMACC). For the first time, I have completed my FAFSA (Free Application for Federal Student Aid). At eighteen years old, I didn't understand that the Department of Education and the government view a veteran's status differently. So, when asked on my FAFSA, "Are you a veteran or do you actively serve in the armed forces?" I clicked the box marked "yes," not realizing that active meant "active duty" and veteran meant "being called up to presidential orders overseas." Regardless, my FAFSA was approved, and my college journey could begin.

The next thing I know, I'm receiving all this money. I mean free money, because of my short and fresh service to our country. Oh, man, I was over the moon. Do you have any idea what it is like to give money to a kid who comes from nothing? Free money that never has to be paid back? It was like $6,000 per semester; it made the difference between focusing on college and not working myself to death. My first semester ends, and everything is great. Decent grades, and I can work my construction job when I have the availability.

The second semester, though, things really took a turn for the worst. Challenge Number 1: I'm intertwined in the most toxic relationship you could ever bear to think of. (Yet, to my own avail, I am taken back to earlier when I said, "I couldn't be the person to hurt someone else." A valuable lesson came from that unfortunate time dating that girl—when it's bad, it doesn't make you wrong to leave respectfully, and how they react is not your weight to carry.) Yes, everything is falling apart, and I am finding myself back amid my own chaos. My grades are slipping, my attendance is slipping, and alcohol is finding me again. I struggled through my second semester and got by with the warning of academic probation. "Damn," I thought. "Okay, I'll work this summer and I'm going to save up money and move to Ankeny. Obviously, living in Indianola and driving forty minutes to school isn't working anymore."

Challenge Number 2: I'm fired from my construction job. Well, it's a great story. Growing up, I always enjoyed construction. As I said earlier, the house I grew up in was built by my great-grandfather, Lodus. My grandfather's name was Lodus Jr. (we referred to him as Grandpa Lodie). Both my great-grandpa and grandfather were men who I would say always carried themselves well. They were big and strong and not too many people squared up with them. My great-grandma and great-grandpa lived right across the driveway from us, so I always learned the ropes of whatever job Lodus Sr. created for himself. My great-grandfather is now gone, but he taught me what working hard looked like. He always believed that if you needed something done, the only time you hire someone else is if you don't have the skills necessary to do it yourself, or the ability to learn it.

Construction isn't a beautiful industry. It's hard work in hot and cold weather. No matter what level you are—from the lowest level to the owner of a multimillion-dollar company—the guys who really know what they are doing are the ones who have put in the hours in the trenches of the construction industry. At the moment, I am in the construction industry as a career. I always tell people, "Anyone can frame a wall, but the difference between knowing how to frame a wall and complying with IBC (International Building Code) while emphasizing customer success in every scenario makes the big difference."

So, at eighteen, when I first started working in construction, it really intrigued me. I learned very quickly that I did not know as much as I thought I did. I started out roofing houses. That's what I did the entire summer of 2014, just before embarking on my journey at DMACC. Roofing is one of the hardest jobs. Especially if you did it the way we did: you had your pallets of shingles dropped as close to your ladder as you could possibly talk the delivery driver into. If you were the lowest man on the totem pole, your job was to carry up shingles for the other teammates. This obviously was right after you spent all morning tearing the old roof off, while the dew-filled morning breeze sprayed your face as you worked.

Dave was my boss, and he was the first man I ever looked up to—someone I thought to myself, "I want my life to be like his." Dave and I had an unspoken connection, as we both shared a similar story from our past. Dave really took me under his wing and did everything he could for me. He saw something in me, something that would take me another handful of years and different milestones to overcome to see in myself.

"You're a man amongst men." I'll never forget Dave telling that to me one afternoon as I was helping him put his newly built shop on his small acreage outside of Des Moines.

I asked, "What does that mean?"

He says to me, "It means if one were to walk into a room full of men, the way you are and the way you carry yourself will always set you apart from the crowd."

I had never thought of myself in that manner, and I would find that message would carry with me as I stepped into the next level.

I learned many lessons while working for Dave. Lessons that, even to this day, I carry with me and find I can draw from my tool belt from time to time. (But I don't wear my tool belt anymore. Insert corny construction business owner joke here.) The greatest lesson he ever taught me was simple: "If it goes against your heart, it's never a good decision." This lesson would come to me in the form of my first firing from Dave.

Anytime someone in my family was in trouble, I was always at their side doing what I could to show I was there for them. I had been missing work because my dad's baby brother (ironically his name is Tyler also)—just a year older than myself—had found himself in the arms of addiction. I received a call from my father that Tyler had overdosed on meth and was in the hospital in Oskaloosa. In that moment, I dropped everything and began my trek to Osky. Just as I was getting to Tyler's room, I realized, there is no Tyler. Well, when one is tweaked out of their mind, Tyler had thought he was being kidnapped by someone and ran away from the hospital. Fortunately, he was scooped up by my father's dad and swiftly brought back to the hospital. Tyler was to remain in the hospital for the next few days for observation. I stayed at Tyler's side while he lay in the hospital, questioning every life decision he had ever made at just barely nineteen years old.

Missing work in construction is never an ideal situation. Your presence is depended on to perform a job within the allotted amount of time given to you by owners, general contractors, or your direct-level boss. The fact I kept calling in to be a part of my broken family really put a damper on Dave's ability to perform the jobs in a timely manner. It wasn't because of my family issues that Dave fired me, but my continual absence.

During that time, I was flown out to Los Angeles to do a photo shoot for Adidas. (No, nothing further ever came of this, nor did I ever see any marketing with my face on it.) For someone from just a small town in Iowa, it really opened my eyes to possibilities. It was a fun time, and I got to meet guys from all around the world.

Before I left, I took my car (I had a red V6 Mustang at the time) to a sketchy car shop while I was gone to get some new tires put on, as every time it rained, the car would be carried all over the road. Being stuck in the lot left my Mustang vulnerable to theft: someone had busted the windows out and stolen my stereo. It was not a good one, but the principle was clear: do not take something that does not belong to you. I wouldn't even know this information until my return from LA. I was paid $2,500 plus all expenses covered to take this trip, so my thought was I would get new tires and use the additional money to cover the cost. Now, I will say the mechanic took care of me. He replaced my window and for my inconvenience, gave me the tires at cost. So, my hat goes off to him. You may have been in a sketchy part of town, but the foundation of your ethical value system doesn't go unnoticed.

Yet again, I face having to call Dave and let him know I wouldn't be at work until Tuesday. I had just missed Thursday and Friday to venture to LA and now I had to miss Monday. I made the call, and for the first time, Dave didn't say much, just "Okay." I could tell by how the conversation was short-lived that it wasn't a good thing for me. Was I right or what?

Ten minutes later, Dave called me and said, "Ya know, Nick, this just isn't working out. You're going to have to find another job. Thanks for your time here and good luck."

My response to Dave was simple: "Dave, thank you for the opportunity. I apologize for putting you in this position. However, can I use you as a reference while I apply for other jobs?"

I know I threw him for a loop. In the construction industry, when you fire someone, there is the unwavering feeling that you're the issue.

A couple hours later, Dave called me again. He said, "Nick, I've been thinking, and firing you doesn't feel right. The job is still yours if you want it."

Obviously, I happily obliged and the lesson that Dave put upon me was "If it goes against your heart, it's probably a bad choice." Not only did I take on the job offer, but I recognized that my reason for being fired was my fault. I had to be the one to make a change, to ensure that I wasn't put in that position again. I made that change, and I continued to work for Dave throughout my first year at DMACC.

Now, I was fired again, and yes, it was again my fault. Dave had a gentleman who worked for him; we always referred to him as "All Veins." Ha! Memories are flooding back. Anyway, Veins and I never saw eye to eye. To him, I was some dumb kid. To me, he was a thirty-something child who underperformed. It was nearing the end of the school year for DMACC, and our task was to roof a house somewhere in the middle of nowhere in Iowa.

In the morning, as we got ready to load the roof with shingles, I began my trek up the ladder to the top of the roof. As I got to the top, Veins apparently thought it would be hilarious to push the ladder straight out as I ascended the top. I didn't find it funny. I freaked out: my safety was in the hands of "All Veins." Veins don't correlate to muscle fiber and your ability to pull back a ladder once you've pushed it past its tipping point.

He had set the ladder back on the rim of the roof. I got down and removed my tool pouches, ready to fight him. Nothing came of it. Dave was on site, and getting into a fight with the homeowner watching is never a good idea. So, I walked it off and found my cool again.

We all got through the day as if nothing happened. I had just climbed into my car, ready to drive back to my apartment, when I found Veins at my driver's window saying, "If you ever come at me like that again, you won't like the outcome. You know I had you and I wouldn't have let that ladder fall."

Let's take a moment to reflect on Veins's internal conflict. This man was upset that some nineteen-year-old kid stood up to him. He let me know he was the dominant one, and I must always know my place in the pecking order.

Well, unfortunately for him, I thrive in conflict (still do). As soon as I stepped out of the car, his finger pressed firmly into my chest and says these words: "You're slow, you're stupid, and you're never going to be anything."

Now, these words burned with an intensity of seven wildfires. I blacked out as soon as he said these words. So, I did the only thing my brain told me to do: We fought in the driveway of the homeowner's house. The one thing you NEVER do in any business industry: fight a coworker in front of a client who is paying you for professional services.

It was over in a flash. I remember we were on the ground and one of the other guys is saying, "Hey, stop, the homeowner's wife just came outside and is on the phone with Dave."

In my moment of anger, I got in my car and sped off. I ripped down the gravel road with all my hurt from those three statements flooding my mind, combining with all the hurts of my past. I see my hammer sticking from my tool bag in my front seat. I grasp it tightly and rip my car into a 180 to beeline as fast I can back to the job site. Upon my arrival back, Veins was on the phone with Dave, making sure he was the first one to tell him his side of the events.

I got out of my car. I squeezed the hammer so tightly in my right hand, I could feel my pulse through my palm as I approached him. The second I got to him, rather than swinging the hammer, I said, "You know what? I'm not slow or stupid, and I am going to do more things and see more places throughout my life than you could ever imagine."

Without saying anything else, I simply turned around and left for good this time.

Then it came, the phone call I knew was gunning toward me. It was Dave and he was pissed. I knew at that moment, there was nothing I could say. I had just done the one unforgivable thing. I was fired and rightfully so. To be honest, this was the beginning of a spiral for me. Not long after that, I struggled to survive.

CHAPTER 13

DO YOUR RESEARCH BEFORE YOU COMMIT

MY FIRST YEAR OF DMACC ENDED AND MY BANK account was almost minus $1,000.00. I am working at a Quick Lane at the local Ford dealership in Indianola. One day, at work, a representative from DMACC contacted me.

"Nick, I need you to send us a letter explaining why you're not listed as dependent on one of your parents on your FAFSA." Weird, but okay. So, I wrote a note on an oil-stained piece of paper and handed it off. DMACC is quiet, so I thought all was good in that realm.

I continue struggling my way through this newfound adult life. But when your bank account is negative, it's hard to pay bills. When you can't pay your rent, you get evicted from your apartment. Luckily, I had made a good friend through my new unit, Jess Fall. Jess was aware of my struggle, and, by the grace of God, his parents were yet another pair of guardian angels sent to my life to help me out in my time of need.

At the beginning of my second year at DMACC, I got a job at the local car shop in Bondurant. My account was back at a positive number (not by much, though). I was ready to begin my second year and get over this hump, so I could get a real job and make something of myself.

There was just one issue. On my first day at DMACC, I received an invoice for the sum of $15,000.00. Once I was able to catch my breath, I immediately raced to the student services center. Ean was the newly appointed Director of Financial Aid. Our first interaction was stressful.

Ean sits me down and he says, "Hey, you incorrectly put that you're a veteran on your financial aid form. So, you owe us that money back."

I just looked at him in confusion and frustration. He wanted me to pay for it then and there.

I said, "There's absolutely no way. I don't have that kind of money."

He requested I take out a loan (yeah right, dude, I don't have any credit). He requested my parents take out a loan and I thought, "Oh yes, maybe my dad can help me." But it was an absolute hard no from my father. His words exactly: "You're going to have to figure this one out on your own." I'll never forget that feeling. It sucked. But he was right. It was my error and I had to fix it.

I returned to Ean with the unfortunate news. By this time, he has seen my oil-stained letter that somehow got lost while DMACC was doing their audit.

He asks me, "You left home at seventeen and your parents don't support you?"

I nod in agreement, and he comes up with this brilliant plan, because of my "extenuating circumstances." He overrides my eligibility for an independent status (that's the status being a veteran gave me in year one) "just to ensure you're getting everything and following along."

The deal from Ean was, "I'm going to give you this money, but you're going to turn around and give it back to us so we can satisfy your debt. To secure our investment, we are going to withhold your transcripts until the account is paid in full."

Ean types out a contract between DMACC and myself, stating that I will give DMACC my Financial Aid to satisfy the debt owed. We both signed it. I thought it was a great idea. The way it was explained made sense and I recognized that I fucked up. I made an honest mistake at a young age. Who hasn't?

But here's where it sucked: I never got that money. The financial situation I was in was agonizing distress. Even living and eating with the Falls (ten minutes from campus), it's hard to strive academically when you can't even afford to make it to class. I chose to focus less on my schooling and more on my employment at the local mechanic shop.

As Dave Ramsey famously puts it, "Treat your debt like a snowball, not an avalanche." I did that, but my short stint at the car shop required me to purchase tools; otherwise, no job. (Shout out to all the mechanics out there.) If I had gone to school, I could only work two days a week. I earned $140 every week. After paying bills, I had no money left over. School suddenly became less important. With an egregious 21 percent interest rate and a $240 a month payment, I was drowning. Credit cards and personal loans went to collections. My whole semester, I lived off credit cards and a personal loan to cover the other loans at the time. (Isn't that a son of a bitch, taking out a loan just to make payments on other loans?) So, I absolutely bombed my third semester. Having already been on academic probation, that was the ticket to being kicked out of college.

Not only was I kicked out, but the idea of going to another college was out the window. (Trust me, I tried.) DMACC withheld my transcripts, so there wasn't much I could do except work to pay the debt that was owed. For three years, my life completely unraveled. I started drinking again. I slept on couches, children's beds, floors. I had more money in collections than I ever had to my name. My service in the military was dwindling; I became known as the "shitbag." (If you serve, then you get it.) It was hell, a nightmare that wouldn't end.

I lived with the Fall family for a year and a half. I left mechanics and went back to what I knew: construction. But there was a problem: I couldn't make more than a laborer because I didn't have a degree. You don't make shit as a laborer. And being in an industry that requires you to provide transportation to the job was tough.

Not to mention the mountain of debt I had accumulated just to survive DMACC. I got to know debt collectors extremely well. I mean so well that I even considered applying to be one at one point. When they called, I could lip-sync their entire spiel before they even began. "My name is X and please know this call is being recorded on a recorded line in the attempt to collect a debt." Even to this day, I remember that sales pitch.

I worked for a company that was based in Des Moines. Mike was the owner; he was a man I looked up to. Mike and I would come to be great friends. He went above and beyond for me regularly. Mike was more than just an employer. He was a person who saw more in me than I could see in myself during a time when I was just trying to survive. Mike would teach me many things in the construction industry that entailed more than just throwing on your pouches and working the daily punch list. I would attend meetings with Mike, and he would tell me this and that about the different components between his construction company and his cleaning company. These conversations and experiences sparked an early interest in me, that maybe I could do the same.

While working for Mike, I thought the answer to my problems would be starting my own company. I failed miserably at that. Ha! So much so, that the IRS audited me, because, well, when you owe taxes, you owe taxes. I had absolutely no idea what I was doing. I knew construction, but I didn't know how to run or operate a business. I would chalk that up to a last-ditch effort at the moment to land a huge job and make so much cash that all my problems would suddenly go away. It most certainly was the worst reason to start a company. I didn't know what an LLC was. I didn't understand, nor did I have any commercial insurance. I was a self-employed cat that operated his "company" out of the trunk of his 2003 Honda Civic. No vision, no goal, no idea what I am doing—except just knowing that I need to do something because I am not making any money doing what I am doing now. After it all came crashing down, my saving grace was that I never quit working for Mike. I would say that's another drag on my first entrepreneurship venture: I wasn't all in on it. If you aren't 100 percent committed, you will never see it through, and that goes for everything in life.

One day, we're gutting a flip home in downtown Des Moines, and Mike walks into the home with a paper from Pella Corporation. He told me they were hiring, and he urged me to apply as they could start me out at enough money to get my life back together. Mike knew my struggles. More importantly, he knew he could no longer offer me what I needed, or in his words, "what I was worth."

He told me, "You apply or don't, but regardless, this is your two-week notice."

I applied and they hired me. I worked at Pella for almost a year and a half (at this point I am just about three years shy of being booted out of DMACC). Mike had it figured out because his plan worked: I got a firm footing on getting my life back together. I am thankful for him seeing so much in me. That is what selflessness looks like, and I strive daily to forge a mentality that it's about you. What can I do for you? Thank you, Mike.

I lived with my father in Oskaloosa during my time at Pella Corporation. To be honest, after being "homeless," moving in with my father felt like a step backward in time. But we must get to where we are trying to go. Well, that wasn't the greatest time for either of us. I always used to say my father and I spend our time best in short stints. The breaking point for me was hard; it took me a few years to get through this one.

Remember when I asked my father to co-sign a loan for me and he told me to "figure it out"? I had recently found out that my dad co-signed a loan for my sister to attend college.

"Why did you kick me out at sixteen and trade me off with Shelby? Why is Shelby worthy of being seen by you, but I am just a burden? What did I do? What did I not do? Again, why can't you just see me?" All these thoughts and feelings flooded me.

Shortly thereafter, I moved in with a coworker from Pella. While I was working at Pella, I befriended another great man, Jeff. Jeff was a broken soul who spent his entire adulthood addicted to drugs and was trying to become a better version of the man he once was. We would hang out at our lunches and sit in his car and smoke cigarettes.

Finally, one day, as I am eating my uncooked ramen noodles with the chicken flavoring sprinkled throughout, he says to me, "Why do you eat ramen every single day?"

I simply replied, "It's all I can afford. I'm working right now to get out of a financial crisis, and all my money (literally all of it) must go to bills."

He replies with a statement I'll never forget: "Man, you're stronger than I could ever dream of being. There's no way I could ever do that."

People don't realize what they say and the impact it can have on you. Even if that statement came from a man who created his own chaos throughout his life, he was just as strong as I was. He too was doing the things necessary to become more than he had always been.

Finally, my life was getting back on track, and I could see the end of the tunnel. We are nearing August 2018, and I had just reenlisted into the military. I never intended to, but the $20,000 reenlistment bonus was beautiful. There was one other thing too: I committed to myself that this time when I reenlist, it's for me. Not to show anyone else I can do it. I reenlisted, and the first half of my bonus hit in early September of that year.

By this time, I had mustered up enough courage to get away from the factory life at Pella. If I stayed because the money was good, I would never get out. Everyone there who was nearing retirement also realized they had spent their entire adult life in a windowless, hot factory. I knew immediately I did not want that. But I also knew I had to do what I had to do.

BH Management hired me to work as a Maintenance Supervisor. The job was not glamorous, but it provided me with an opportunity to get back into what I always loved: construction. Being a maintenance guy in an apartment complex brings a multitude of different construction problems that need solutions. Moreover, the idea I could lead other people intrigued me. I thought it would be good for me to take this chance. Not only that, but it gave me the opportunity to get back to Des Moines. My newfound career began, and I was nearing the end of all my collections. The bonus money was a huge supplement and gave me a good cushion while I started this new journey. Little did I know this new journey would take a hard turn, and rather quickly.

CHAPTER 14

REBIRTH

BEFORE WE GET TOO FAR DOWN THE RABBIT HOLE with this story, I want it to be known that I am not even hinting at the fact that DMACC or any of its representatives are guilty of the events that will occur throughout the next few chapters. This is my truth of the events that happened to me; this is my story to tell. I do not wish to persuade any reader.

It's November 2018, and everything is going great. My new job is good. I am coming up with a plan to pay my last owed debt, DMACC. I had just walked into an apartment to prepare it for incoming tenants (we called these services "sparkle shines"), and I receive a phone call. It is a representative from CBE calling to collect a debt. However, this call was unlike any other debt collector call I had ever received. The conversation was brief. "Hi Nick, this is X from CBE. We have just received an account from DMACC, and you have until December to pay the account in full or else."

Woof, these guys are for real. I explained to the lady that I'm working to pay it off now, but I don't have the money to give in a lump sum. She responds by telling me to figure it out, "get a loan if you have to," and hangs up. Luckily, I had become friends with my banker. He knew I had hit some snags and was working to right the wrongs I had created for myself. Maybe he could help me, as he knows me; he knows that, through hell or high water, I will satisfy the debt owed. I met with him at his office after my phone call with CBE. This is where my whole world would begin to be turned upside down.

I caught up with him in his office. Ten minutes into our conversation, he leans back in his chair and says these words: "Uhhh, woah. Okay. I'm not a lawyer. But before you and I have a further conversation, I want you to call this attorney and see what he says. If he thinks it's legit, then come back and I will do everything I can to help you. But it's out of my hands once we file the credit application." He knew I had shit credit.

I call this guy. He was an attorney for a finance company in downtown Des Moines. I assumed since he knew finance law, my banker thought he would have an idea about what is going on. He has a chuckle and says, "Oh, no, if this went down the way you're saying it did, they've got to eat that." It was his recommendation that I speak to an accounting specialist at DMACC and see if I can get a better understanding.

I met with Ann at the end of November. The intention of the meeting was to come up with a payment system so DMACC would remove my account from collections. I would contract to pay $725.00 a month, which would satisfy the balance in a year. But she added, "If you just give me $20.00 a month, I will keep your account out of collections." I requested my account printout. There was a problem: "It's inaccessible. Your account is in a separate system, and I can't access that."

"What? You're literally the account manager. Maybe you could just type in my student ID number and print it out?"

No, no, she couldn't.

You know what I got from that meeting? I got the first hint this was wrong from the beginning. The way Ean was with me three years ago, back in 2015—the way everything played out. Three years ago, I was told, "You made a mistake, and you owe this money. In the interest of the higher education system, we must secure our investment, so we're going to withhold your transcripts until your debt owed to us is paid in full. Sorry about your luck, kid."

The weight of carrying this burden for three years, just to realize I had gotten fucked. The amount of rage that comes with that I wouldn't wish upon my greatest enemy. It is that kind of rage that makes men do ungodly things. The last three years of my struggle, the last three years of my fight to survive, was because *they* made the fucking error? Not me? I carried that mistake; even more so, I owned it. For years, when people would ask me why I didn't finish school, I would tell them, "I made a mistake on my FAFSA. It's a complicated situation, but I am working to get back there." When you bear a weight and then learn that maybe it was never yours to bear, words cannot express what that does to a person in that moment.

I made an error. I incorrectly checked the box on my FAFSA, saying I was a veteran, when in the Department's view, I was not. I own that, and I also own that it was an honest mistake. But I refuse to carry the weight of how my institution handled their part. It's my decision not to carry that weight, but it is not my right to say they did it wrong; that's their choice.

I had drill that weekend and my mind wandered into the unknown of "What the hell is going on?" My mind had begun to break. I was spending all my free time researching, calling, speaking to whoever could just give me some type of insight. After hopping from rabbit hole to rabbit hole, I learned this from the website of the Department of Veterans Affairs: "At any time when a student selects that they are a veteran on the FAFSA, that answer is then automatically sent to a nationwide database where it is either confirmed or denied. However, to remove liability, the government requires every college that receives additional benefits for veteran students to do one last check and either confirm or deny the student is in fact a veteran; no such liability will be placed on the student." Following that, I learned many colleges have a third-party company verify status as they don't want to carry that liability either. Moreover, I learned that DMACC had done their own check.

I set up a meeting with Ean. I figured, after our meetings three years ago, he would square this away and straighten everything out. I opened the meeting with one question: "Who confirmed my Veteran's status at DMACC? Since someone here did, why is this debt mine to pay?" Ean was very cautious about what he said. For me, that was all I needed to believe; it was what I had already surmised.

The next day, on December 4, 2018, the debts that had been the bane of my life, that were aggressively attempting to be collected by CBE and DMACC, were paid in full by DMACC. Just like that, it was paid. Furthermore, my transcripts were finally released. My life unraveled down a path of rage, chaos, darkness, pain, and the unknown.

After that meeting with Ean, I lost my mind. I set meetings. I made phone calls. I emailed everyone. I even called the governor's office. Some innocent intern answered the phone and all I could say was this: "My name is Nick Darland

and I'm in the National Guard. If I find out I've been getting fucked by my college for the last three years, then I am going to absolutely lose my mind." Ha! I feel bad for that girl! She just responds with, "Uhm, okay, well, I'm sorry you're going through this," in the sweetest "this dude is insane" tone.

I'm aggressively researching. I am aggressively fighting. Fighting for what I believe is right and for the truth. I contact the US Department of Education and file an investigation with the "Ombudsmen Group." Which didn't much appreciate my personal investigative style for contacting them daily about updates I believed I had found. Local authorities, US Department of Education Inspector General's Office, and finally, the Secretary of Education herself. I beat down any wall that was in my way, and I didn't care what your title was, your social status, even more so, your political affiliation. I wanted answers. I was stuck in chaos, and I was becoming a monster.

DMACC had paid my debts, and I could return and get my degree, yet it wasn't that simple for me. You must understand the unfathomable rage that I was experiencing. The anger shook me to my core. I had to channel that, and the best way I knew how to do that was to figure it out. For me, it was about the principle. I had never been so determined to bulldoze through anything in my life, and my resolve set me on the path of what I now like to call rebirth. Otherwise, I don't believe I would be writing this story.

I lost my mind completely, and the more I dove into it, the more enraged I became. I needed a lawyer, and this was not easy to come by. Now, I didn't realize that different attorneys do different things. The first lawyer I spoke to was primarily a tax attorney, so you can imagine his confusion when I strolled into his office with a blue legal binder full of federal codes and regulations. He was very intrigued by the entire story. Every attorney I approached primarily said the same thing: "There's something here, but I don't even know how to approach this." Eventually, I had everything figured out. Every law is burned in the depths of my mind. If you had met me, you would have thought I was an attorney.

We're now in January and I've gone from 220 to 167 pounds in a couple of months. Feeling hopeless is a dangerous place to be. Every day gets darker and darker, no matter how brightly the sun shines. I don't know what else to do, so I call Military One Source, which is a program for struggling service members. An operator answers the phone and I just lose every sense of my composure. Struggling to release any words from my mouth, I just cry in a way I never knew I was capable of. The sudden release of emotions rendered up many red flags on this poor operator's radar, and in that moment, he just talked to me, reassuring me he was there for me and would make it a priority to get me in front of someone fast. Following that conversation, this gentleman would call me daily with updates for about two weeks.

Wow, the power of that last paragraph. I'm in tears as I type these words because I relive that morning. The pain I had coursing through my heart was truly unbearable. The operator could sense my state of urgency. He stayed on the phone with me and talked me through my emotional outburst. The dude wasn't a therapist, but he had the greatest impact on me that morning—he just listened to me. He let me navigate my thoughts and emotions. At the end of it, he said, "I'm going to work to get you in front of the right person. You hang in there and stay strong." There is an old saying, "You never know how strong you are until being strong is the only option you have." There's so much truth to that, no matter what you do or what you're going through. Please know you are stronger and capable beyond measure. There was never any luck getting me in front of a therapist, and that sucked, because I really needed one.

I was at the end of my rope. I knew I was done. It was time. If life sucks this much, and all you do is endure one shitty event after another, then I don't want to live anymore. I gave it my best; my best was not enough. So, it's time for me to speak to God and ask him, "What the fuck, man?" Turns out, I didn't have to die for God to hear me.

I made a commitment. I had bought a gun at my local sportsman's store. But I didn't have a permit to carry, so there was a twenty-four-hour hold on it while they did all their checks. I thought to myself, "Well, this works. I'll go out tomorrow. Tonight, I am going to go to both my parents' houses and tell them everything they did to hurt me growing up, and that I had forgiven them."

My father was up first. I showed up at his house on a chilly January night, and I walked in unannounced. I sat him at his kitchen table, I looked him in the eyes, and I told him everything he did that broke my heart throughout my whole life. However, the second part of my plan changed at that moment. Instead of saying "I forgive you," I looked him in the eyes and said, "Because of you, I will do more, be more, and become more." I stood up, and for the first time, as a man, I shook his hand, looked him in the eyes and said, "Thank you."

My mother and stepdad were next. I made the trek to their house in Knoxville. I gave them the speech I had just given my father. My stepdad hugged me and we both cried. I could sincerely feel this weight lifted off my shoulders as we held each other. For the first time in my life, we were just two men who chose love. It was beautiful and I cherish that moment. My mother, however, has never been good at hearing the things she's done wrong. She kicked me out, and I had been in enough fights with my mother throughout the years that I knew an object was coming my way. I walked fast to the door. Just as I had called it, a brad nailer comes hurtling toward me.

For me, that was taking control of my internal monster. You see, I finally took responsibility for my life. There was no more blaming anyone but me. Not my parents, not DMACC, not my environment. I learned that when you blame something, that's where you put the power. For the first time, the power was mine and only mine. For me, that was the "pivotal moment." That was God talking to me, without me having to kill myself for us to have that conversation. I thank God for that moment, regularly.

Luckily, my life had conditioned me not only to step into this, but to what I now attribute to the grace of God, to continue to endure it. Whether I could ever get over it was something I didn't know. But I kept moving on and doing what I could. January 2019 would be when the old Nick dies and the Nick that writes to you today begins to be born. It was the end of Nick, the victim, and the beginning of Nick who holds his own power. It would just take some time for me to fully realize that.

CHAPTER 15

THERAPY (AND HOSPITALS) SAVE LIVES

NOT MUCH LONGER AFTER HAVING RECKONED WITH my parents, I attended drill at Camp Dodge. It was our annual PHA's (Periodic Health Assessment). Drill weekends had become an opportunity for everyone to witness my chaos unfold. Everyone thought I was crazy, and rightfully so, down this path of self-righteous implosion.

I remember waking up on Sunday morning and just feeling off. I had become accustomed to this feeling, as every day was an off-day for me. However, this time, I knew something was wrong. As I crawled out of my bunk, I stumbled to the DFACC for our morning chow. Food and I were in a bad relationship at this time, so I ate little. What I did, however, was end up back in my bunk and drift back to sleep until noon that day.

If you're in the military, none of us get the right just to go back to bed. To this day, I think my unit was watching me implode; they must have thought it's best to just let Darland sleep. It was the most sleep I had gotten in months, and it didn't help. When I woke up, I was utterly discombobulated. I had no idea where I was; all I can remember doing was walking aimlessly around Camp Dodge. Hell, I ended up on the complete opposite side of the post. That was until a van pulled up behind me, and two full-bird colonels swooped me up. They asked me what I was doing. I let them both know I was here attending the PHA event. They insisted I hop in the van, and they would get me to where I needed to go.

"Oh, well, sirs, now that I have a moment of your time, let me tell you about the project I'm working on right now." Ha! I did that, and the second I opened my mouth, they couldn't get me across the post fast enough. They dropped me off at S70, and the one bird in the passenger seat just looks at me and says, "Good luck, troop."

"Troop," oh, I kind of like that. To this day, I refer to my junior enlisted and lower NCOs as troops.

I attended the PHA event and mustered my way through. When I was done, I got to the help desk to turn in my packet. The lady looks at it, looks at me, and says, "Oh, you're not done, SPC. Go see Behavioral Health."

Shocked and confused, I approach SFC Konrad. "Hey, what's up with this?" I ask.

He replies, "Yeah, it's above my pay grade, but we're concerned about you. For a lack of better words, you go see Behavioral Health or we're going to process you out of the military."

Okay.

My initial therapy session was short, simple, and sweet. The first words that came out of my mouth: "Sir, I'm fine. Everything is fine. I don't need this."

Turns out, those words push-started a semi-truck of the kind therapists use for "How bad do you need therapy?" A simple statement like that will take you off the charts. I spent most of the evening in that office, and the LTC just sits back, sighs, and says, "I am going to refer you to someone else. There isn't enough time in this day for you and me to walk through this."

They sent me back to the barracks, where I collapsed in agonizing pain. To this day, it was the worst pain I could ever imagine. I was sweaty, clammy, and I smelled like ass. My leadership came, and off to the VA Hospital I went. They did an emergency CT scan and found that my appendix had ruptured and was leaking. (I had to drink that chalk shit and wow, it was disgusting.) They rushed me into emergency surgery.

When I woke up the next morning, my company commander and my Warrant Officer walked into the room to check on me. My commander says, "Hey, we got hold of your family. Where is everyone?"

I knew immediately no one came. I responded, gasping, while tears began to waterfall, "No one showed up."

That's it, that's all I could say. I believe at that moment, my leadership learned that there is much more to SPC Darland than just this DMACC shit. My commander, frustrated and questioning how no one from my family could be there, makes a phone call and demands that a chaplain come to the VA and sit with me.

Chaplain Craig would turn out to be one of my biggest cheerleaders. As soon as he walks into the room, I've got him. "Hey, let me tell you about what I'm dealing with right now."

He was blown away, for what he thought was just going to be a visit with a troop in the hospital turned into a three-hour conversation, followed by awe.

My orders were to stay in the hospital for two days, so they could pump me full of antibiotics to prevent the sepsis from getting worse. I happily obliged. For the first time in a couple of months, I stayed in bed, had meals catered to me, and I researched as many laws as I could. At that time, you couldn't have given me a better plan.

An NCO, SSG Davis, from my unit drove up to take me home from the hospital. When he arrived, I was out of bed and ready to go. I was abruptly stopped by the nurse, who said, "You have to be wheelchaired out. It's hospital policy."

I looked at her, and I said, "I walked into this hospital. I'll walk out of it."

In that moment, I believe she was in so much shock at the response that she allowed me to walk out of the hospital. I believe that in a funny cosmic way, by me doing that, it had given me some sense of power.

Well, here we are, one step forward and seven steps back. (Is that a song?) I had just rekindled with my family. Now we're all back to square one, but this time, it's different. I had given myself the power of all the pain that had been caused. So, even though waking up in a hospital bed after surgery and realizing that not one family member was there hurt badly, I swiftly moved past the drama. That's the crazy thing about power: when it's yours, it's truly yours. Find your power.

During my time off work, I find myself plunked in front of a therapist, Jeff Scott. I'll never forget that first interaction with him. I told Jeff the same speech as I told the LTC. He asked me one question: "I hear you, but how are you doing?"

Oh, hold on, Jeff. What are you doing right now? And there it was. It felt as if all my trauma suddenly disappeared, like a helicopter dropping water on a forest fire.

I paused for a moment, and the only response I could give him was to just cry. That's all I did. And you know what Jeff did? He sat there and let me cry. When I was ready to talk, he just let me talk. He didn't listen to respond; he listened just to listen. That was Jeff's power. Listen to listen, not to respond. My wife will happily agree with my statement there.

Therapy saved my life, truly. Even to this day, as I write this chapter, I attended a good session with my therapist last night. The dynamic has changed over the years. It's gone from learning how to navigate trauma to telling my therapist, "Well, I started Harvard Business School last week, and oh yeah, I'm writing a book." He just laughs and says, "Yes, yes, you are, because what else would Nick be doing?" Ha!

It is now the beginning of February, and I am just getting back to work from my surgery. I am still speaking with Jeff multiple times a week, but there's one issue: I'm broke, and short-term disability doesn't pay shit. The cushion I had saved up had now been drained on rent and groceries.

I asked my father if he could help me out financially. This is shortly after my hospital stay and after the reckoning with my parents. He says the same thing he had said so many times before: "Son, you're going to have to figure this one out. I can't help you." In that moment, I fully understood that I don't need this man in my life. For far too long, I have done everything I can to be seen by this one person. I had given him the power of my acceptance. For the first time, I was okay with him telling me no, because this would be the last time I would ever put myself in that position.

I let my father go. I did it for me. I wasn't a child anymore; I was a man. For months, I didn't talk to my father. I'll never forget when my wife and I first met. She asked me if she would ever meet my dad. I told her, "No, he's not a part of my life and I'm okay with that." It would be my sister who would reach out to me in May of that year, inviting me to a barbecue that my dad was having. It would be my wife that would convince me I needed to go. My wife, in that moment, showed me the power of letting go and forgiveness. I firmly believe this was the moment that allowed me to recover.

Being off work, and now creeping into February, I find myself with some light in my darkness. I am still bulldozing my way through everything. I finally have my day with the President of DMACC. There is just one issue: I don't yet have an attorney. I knew if I attended that meeting with no representation, they would never take me seriously. But I am determined through hell or high water to attend this meeting and get some answers. I found Matt Sahag, with Dickey, Campbell & Sahag PLC. For the first time, I have an attorney who doesn't have a conflict of interest and is qualified to take on my case. Matt specialized in accounting law. It took me less than ten minutes in that first meeting to explain what was happening before he agreed to represent me.

The next week, we met at DMACC and sat with President Rob Denson and Denny Presnall (Ankeny's appointed board member). The funny thing was, in the meeting, I was so well versed in everything that I did all the talking. I explained it to these guys step by step. Matt sat in the chair to the right of me and drew circles and squares the whole time. I knew in that meeting I had made a large impact on both Rob and Denny. Pride filled the air. It was enough for me to keep moving forward. I'll never forget Denny leaning back in his chair just flabbergasted by what he had just sat through. He stood up in shock, shook my hand, and complimented me on how smart I was. It was a warm moment for me, I'll admit that.

Matt had gotten to work and really started taking my blue legal binder seriously. (I wouldn't even leave it in my car because I had this fear that it would go missing, and all my research would be gone.) He says, "Nick, I've spoken with my partners, and yeah, there is something here. If there wasn't, people like Rob and Denny wouldn't take time out of their day to meet with you. They're just too busy." From there, Matt took over the case and I could move on with my life.

It was not as easy as me handing over my blue legal binder to Matt and saying, "It's yours now." In the meantime, I was calling, texting, emailing him regularly with newfound updates, theories, and questions. Matt was always supportive and always made an effort to ensure I was heard; it was a wonderful gesture I still carry today. Matt filed a lawsuit, which was later moved to Federal Court. Now that Matt was in the driver's seat, and I was working hard to not be a passenger driver, I focused my attention on getting my life back on track.

CHAPTER 16

MY REASONS WHY

WITH MATT ON MY SIDE, AND REGULARLY REMINDING me to let him do what I have hired him to do, I decided it's time to move forward. I downloaded the Tinder App and I match with this cute girl named Taylor. Today, I tell people I met Taylor in the "midst of chaos."

I'll never forget our first date: February 17, 2019. It was a Sunday, and I had just taken my little brother Jesse home after he spent the weekend with me. I remember when I went to pick her up; I was driving a loaner. My actual car was a 2016 Dodge Dart Rallye Sport (those are basically the old Neons you may remember from the 90s). It was nothing exquisite and the interest rate was egregious (15 percent), but it was mine and it was the first thing I got on my own. So, I was proud. Unfortunately, in Iowa, we get snow, and a racecar like a Dodge Dart doesn't handle well on slick roads; I had a run-in with a curb. The only vehicle the dealer had for me was a 2018 Dodge Ram 1500 Crew Cab Big Horn. Um, yes, please! I did have a conversation with myself on the way to get Taylor. "Do I tell her it's a loaner? Is that weird if I do?" I concluded, "Well, it does have Illinois license plates. So, if she asks, then I'll tell her." Well, she never asked. Nor did she acknowledge she was going on a first date with a guy whose truck was from Illinois.

We had our first date at Buzzard Billy's in downtown Des Moines. During our entire first date, all I could do was tell Taylor how I wanted to travel the world. I want to do this. I want to do that. I want to impact people. She responds in a quiet voice and says, "I've always just wanted a cute house, in a small town with a wraparound porch and a fenced-in yard." In that moment, my mind said, "I could do that." That's when I knew this beautiful, blue-eyed, blonde-haired woman, who was playing with her chicken strips while I inhaled my bowl of gumbo, would be the woman I married.

I received a call from the dealership where my car was being worked on, that the Ram they had loaned had a recall. Sad, I returned the truck. Upon my arrival, the lady handed me a key to a brand-new Camaro and said, "I'm sorry, this is all we have last minute." Uhm, no need to apologize lady, I'll take it!

I drove to Taylor's parents to pick her up so we could begin our night. She got in my car, and she immediately looked at me and said, "Okay, what do you do? Are you a low-key drug dealer?"

I responded, "Oh, no, the truck had a recall, so I had to take it back. This is a loaner." Praying internally that the conversation stopped there. It didn't.

She said, "Oh well, when do you think you'll get your truck back?"

"Yeah, that was a loaner, too."

It's out. I finally said it, and the weight of my own lying was finally released.

She said, "Well, what do you drive then? And where is your actual car?"

"Well, I drive a 2016 Dodge Dart Rallye and I got into an accident the weekend before we met, so it's being repaired."

"Oh, you mean like one of those Neon kinds of cars?"

Gasping for air and releasing my withheld humility, I say, "Yes, it's like one of the Neons, but it's a Rallye and it's cool." Ha!

The car wasn't cool. It was awful. I finally traded that car for a 2020 Chevy Silverado RST. But to my surprise, I was sad when I had to let go of the "ol' dartsky." That car and I had been through a lot together; we had in some weird way bonded over time. With luck, some good soul ended up with it.

During my chaos, I went to a church that is local to Des Moines. Taylor, never much of a churchgoer, attended my Monday night service with me. After the service, we returned to my car (I got the Dart back). She says, "I just think that if you're a good person and treat people well, then you'll be just fine." My wife listens to a lot of heavy raps as a Special Ed teacher; she was born to do what she does. (I'm serious, I couldn't do it. No way.) But she does, and she is the best at what she does. Meeting her, you would never know it; she displays herself as this small-town girl with nothing but innocence raining upon her. But listen carefully: her subwoofer is always bumpin'!

I don't attend church anymore. I am a firm believer in God, and I have seen His working in my life and others that can't be expressed by any other human hand. However, I don't believe I need to raise my hand in the air every Sunday. My faith is mine and mine alone to carry.

Taylor and I had been dating for a year and a few months now. I am working full time at Camp Dodge, and everything is coming together. DMACC stuff is still going on, but it's in Matt's hands. Taylor and I started discussing moving in together. Now, mind you, I had never lived with a female, so I was nervous. However, I realize I am about to propose to her and so it all makes sense. I had done my due diligence and asked her parents for their approval, which they happily granted me. (When I asked her parents, her dad said I must promise never to give her back and her mom wanted two goats. Both of which, at the time, I thought were more than fair trades.)

I bought a ring and everything is great; I have the entire proposal planned out. It's big, it's beautiful, it's crazy. But then COVID-19 hits and the entire world shuts down; literally the day I planned to pick up Taylor's ring from the jewelry shop, it closed. I had no idea what to do, so my future mother-in-law says, "Well, just get a temporary ring from Amazon, T would understand." (T is what her parents call her.) I took the advice and ordered a temporary ring. Taylor and I are moving the last of my things to our new condo. I checked the mail at my old address for the last time and lo and behold, the damn ring is right there. I freak out. I wasn't expecting this! How do I hide it, so she doesn't see it?

In a haste to hide it, I threw the package in the side pocket of my driver's door and off we go to the new apartment. We hit the interstate and my whole life is flashing before my eyes. I'm grasping the steering wheel in a fret of what feels like surviving. To the best of my ability, I can only ask Taylor one question: "So what's your timeline, like with us?" Oh God, what a bad question to ask a girl who already knows you're the man she's going to marry. She spews dates and goals. All I could do was grab the ring, slap it on the center console, and say, "Well, you wanna get married?" If you know my wife and me, then you'll say, "Yeah, that checks out. That's exactly what Nick would do." Ha! We got engaged on Interstate 235 heading North toward Ankeny and it was beautiful in our own way.

Taylor and I have been happily together for five years and married for going on three. I gave her that beautiful house in a small town. I couldn't get the wraparound porch, nor do I want a fenced-in yard, primarily because I'll lose my mind dealing with the weeds. But that's the beautiful thing about marriage. It's full of compromises. My wife is an absolute saint for dealing with me daily. I have become a person of what I like to call "productive adversity." I am constantly doing this: putting myself into situations that are going to challenge me and force me to grow. I love it; it's a pursuit I will never stop.

The second part of my love are my daughters, Andi Grace and Faithlyn Rose. The day Andi was born was the first time in my life I cried tears of pure joy. I never thought I could love another human being so deeply the way I love this little girl. I looked at her for the first time and I promised to her out loud, "I promise to give you the best life I possibly can." I am committed to keeping that promise every single day.

When we found out Andi was a girl, I was happy and excited. Taylor had already had Andi's name picked out and I had no say whatsoever. I am glad because she is most certainly an Andi. Taylor let me have the middle name though, and I knew immediately I wanted it to be Grace. Grace because I knew this little girl was the gift to me from the life I have endured by the Grace of God. Everything I endured, every trial, error, moment of forgiveness, strength, and weakness, brought me to that little girl. I would do it all over again 10,000 times if that meant the outcome was Andi.

Our youngest daughter, Faithlyn, passed away and it is a feeling I wouldn't wish on anybody. Faithlyn passed from what is called a "fetal death," (meaning she passed away before the pregnancy came to full term). Taylor and I were scheduled to attend our anatomy appointment. It was a beautiful day, and I was running late to the appointment, so I called to ensure Taylor knew I was on my way and to wait.

Taylor wanted a boy, and I was praying for a girl. After having Andi and watching her grow, there is something about being a girl dad, that just really excites me. Maybe I fear if I have a boy, I will be too hard on him. I don't know, to be honest. The day is going great, and we are both excited to find out who is right. We get to the procedure room and the ultrasound tech begins her procedure, not long after starting, she silently puts away her things and asks us to wait until she returns. Taylor and I didn't think anything of it in the moment; it wasn't until the doctor returned to the room with a look of deep sorrow on his face.

I am no clinical psychologist, but not much has to be said when you sense the grief of another. The doctor who approached us with the unfortunate news was the same doctor who worked with us the entire time my wife was pregnant with Andi and performed the delivery of Andi. So, he was very familiar with who we were.

I wish I could sit here and tell you that all my life experiences up until this point have conditioned me for an event like this. As if I could muster through my forest of wisdom, knowledge, and experience to come up with an answer on how I could solve this problem, but I couldn't. All I could do was sit there and watch as my wife broke into pieces, mourning the loss of the child we were both so eager to meet. I had to muster every ounce of strength within me in those moments to stay calm and collected while the doctor continued giving us the appropriate support and information we both needed in that moment. The worst part of it, since Taylor was so far along with Faithlyn, she still had to give birth.

The procedure for an unfortunate event such as this is called a "D&E" (dilation and evacuation). It takes a special team of doctors under certain conditions to be able to successfully perform this procedure so there is minimal risk posed to the mother. For Taylor and me, our procedure wouldn't happen for another week after finding out the news of the loss of our daughter. And that was yet another experience that I just had absolutely zero answer to. It was as if the entire afternoon was a bad dream, and we were both waiting to wake up.

The morning of the procedure was a daunting one. On one hand, Taylor and I are both ready for this, so we can really begin the grieving and moving forward process. It was hard to do that in that week because it didn't seem real. If you saw my wife, you saw she was pregnant. They wheeled Taylor back to her operation room, and I was asked to wait out in the waiting room until the doctor was ready to speak with me. About an hour later, I was asked to come back to the consulting room and wait for the doctor.

As I sit in this small room awaiting the doctor for an update, I find myself overwhelmed with thoughts and feelings. Not long after waiting, the doctor comes in and sits next to me and speaks in a light mournful tone. "The procedure went well, and Taylor should be in recovery here shortly. I know last week, we couldn't give you the gender due to the circumstances, but I thought I would let you know it's a girl." My heart drops, and all I can do in that moment is just be still, thank the doctor for everything, and ask him that I be the one to tell Taylor that we had a little girl.

I am escorted back to the recovery room, where I sit and wait for my wife to be wheeled in from her procedure, I will never forget the look on her face as they brought her in. It was purely a look of defeat. As a husband, and as a father, we think of ourselves as the protector of our family (at least I do anyway), and throughout this whole week-long process, I felt like I failed. I couldn't do much for my wife, I couldn't do anything for my daughter who was now gone. It was a whirlwind of a week. All I could do was just be there, and by doing so, I learned that more times than not, that is all that is needed.

Taylor and I opted to get Faithlyn cremated, I will never forget the day I was at the office and Taylor called to tell me that Faithlyn was ready to be picked up from the funeral home. It was the first time I got to hold my daughter, and she was sealed away in an urn. However, I have concluded that although my daughter never got a full shot at life, that doesn't mean she never has to live. So, I have chosen to share the condensed version of what happened in the idea that Faithlyn will forever live on through my family and through this book.

To any parent out there who has lost a child—whether fetal, infant, child, or adult—I am deeply sorry for your loss. It is a void that, no matter what, can never be filled. It is as if for the rest of time a piece of your soul will forever be missing. Hold your loved ones tight and forgive as much as you can, and always say I love you because time is rented, not bought.

CHAPTER 17

HOMEREVISIONS, LLC

TAYLOR KNEW I WASN'T HAPPY WORKING FOR SOMEone else. You would think I would never leave my cushy job at Camp Dodge, but it was the same thing every day. Wake up, go to the gym, do my duties for the day, come home, and do it all again the next day. There was no challenge. There was no requirement for a better me. The excitement and sense of self-worth was slowly dwindling. As I had tossed around the idea of starting a company, one day we were in Home Depot. Taylor knew I was itching to do something big, so she told me to start my own construction company. On August 5, 2020, HomeRevisions was born.

Being the owner of HomeRevisions was my personal step into being the man that is writing this story for you today. The name of the company has deep meaning for me. "Home" is for my family, and our homeowners, and promising always to provide a place of safety and comfort. And "Revisions"—just as my life was once broken and ugly, but has now been revised into something strong, powerful, and beautiful, just so we are always taking broken houses and making them beautiful again.

The few clients I represent in this story convey a clear message: some companies adhere to their expertise, while other relentlessly pursue every opportunity. HomeRevisions started out chasing anything and everything. Throughout my time owning HR, I found inspiration from every client I have worked for. Whether the situation has been good or bad, I learned a lesson from each one.

Looking back, it feels as though everything I endured throughout my life brought me to this moment. Who I am today are the people who surround me daily in my professional and personal life. Not to mention where I continue to strive to go and to become. HR was no easy task, and it still isn't, but in the famous words of Zig Ziglar, "You don't build a business. You build people, and the people build the business." That was something I was doing before I even heard that quote. However, I can assure you it rang volumes when I did.

People ask me constantly, "How did you become so successful so quickly?" Well, I didn't gain success quickly. It took me a lifetime, with many mountains to overcome. I treat my companies, my personal life, and my career in the military, saying, "It's all about the people." As a business owner, I say my role in life is to make critically calculated decisions for the betterment of my people. That's our primary core value; internally we call it "P&P" ("Protect and Provide"). We protect every homeowner from unworkmanlike craftsmanship. We are committed to providing a superior service driven by quality, integrity, and constant growth.

At HR, our motto is, "You supply the vision; we supply the rest." My leadership team makes most of the decisions, and my role is primarily advisory. *In my personal life, my wife makes all the decisions, and I don't get to be an advisor.* Finally, in the military, I decided at "the capacity at which your career can handle." You could say the different adversities I endured developed a mindset that the hard things don't seem so hard anymore—it's all just life. However, focusing on the people and embracing our core values in everything we do will always project us forward. When you go against your core, you go against what is wrong in your own eyes.

HomeRevisions started out as me doing side jobs (as I am sure most construction companies do). I would work nights and weekends doing a variety of tasks for anyone who would hire me. I will never forget the time I was hired by an office in Des Moines, to put twenty desks together. I had worked on this throughout the week and by Friday, I only had three desks left. However, over the weekend, I had to go to drill. At the time, I had drilled in Davenport. So, the idea that I could do the remaining three on Saturday after drill was unrealistic as Davenport is almost a three-hour drive from Des Moines. Staying true to my word about having the desks done and set by open of business that Monday left me with the only choice of finishing the last three desks when I returned home from drill that Sunday night. By the time I had returned to Des Moines, It was almost 7:00 p.m., as soon as I got home, I changed out of my service uniform and went directly to their office. My wife even assisted me. Until 3:00 a.m., I assembled these desks to ensure I met my timeline and satisfied the client—just to go home, shower, and get ready to be at work at Camp Dodge by 6:00 a.m.

It was frustrating, hard work, and never knowing where the next job would come from. Until the next job came from referrals. Referral after referral, I got so many calls from people that it was overwhelming. I'll never forget that day at Camp Dodge, my senior NCO, SFC Erlemeier, pulled me outside and said, "I can't have you coming into work anymore and focusing on your company. You may need to decide what you want here." He insisted I take the step and do my company full time, followed by reassurance that if things didn't work out, I would always have my job at Camp Dodge.

I gave my two-week notice, and I set out to step into what will be the next version of myself: Nick, the business owner. It was no easy task, but as I was going through it, it didn't seem bad. Turns out, life had conditioned me to be very comfortable being uncomfortable. I must thank my wife, truly. Without her support, I don't know where I would be today, and I don't just mean being a business owner. I mean every step of the way since we first met. When I was going through my DMACC stuff, it was her constant, "At some point, you have to let this go and move on." Even in my early days of the company, I would daydream, and I would dream hard. She was always there to bring me back to reality. She still is. She is the ying to my yang.

I am still hardheaded and take on things that are hard, constantly. I attribute that to the success of my companies. My companies are successful because I choose to be successful. I choose the hard path, the path less traveled. Not only do I choose the hard things, but I choose the people. Invest in yourself, invest in others. You don't build businesses; you build people and then people build the businesses. That's the second time now I have written that. So, hint, hint.

My first job full time with HR was repairing a roof rim on a garage in Colfax where a tree had fallen onto the gable ladder and crushed it right below the peak. I had done enough side jobs that I could hire my first employee, Kevin, who is Kolton's little brother. Kevin was my first employee, and today he is my office manager. He's been with me since day one and he is also a member of our leadership team. Kevin was going to school at Iowa State at the time with the dream of being an ag teacher. Well, to everyone's surprise, after the first summer of him working with me, he switched his major because he fell in love with the industry.

We fixed the gable ladder, and I felt a sense of pride, because I could teach Kevin a thing or two. The client was so pleased. We had also gotten to know each other. As we were packing up, he took me to his garage, and inside are boxes and boxes of brand-new DeWalt tools. A miter box saw, a table saw, clamps. Literally, a contractor's start-up package. He hands me the money I am owed for performing the repairs on his home.

He says, "I hope you know you're going to be somebody. I can just feel it. I want you to have these tools."

I responded, "I can't take these. I appreciate the offer, but if I am going to be successful, let me pave that path myself."

I'll never forget his response. "Your success is going to be attributed to the people and the things you do for them, and that they do for you. Take them."

Kevin and I loaded up the truck and off we went. To our first homeowner, thank you. I attribute a part of our success to your generosity that day.

A much larger job was a house in Grinnell. For a year, the homeowners had attempted to find a company to take on their project, but no one wanted it. They owned a large Sears & Roebuck catalogue craftsman-style home, and this thing is a monster. An absolute display of status for its day. They needed new fascia and soffit all the way around their home. The job sounds simple, but it was not. Nervously, I met with the homeowner, and we connected. I could sense their desire to get their home fixed so they could move on with their life. I also could sense they had lost hope of ever finding a contractor. I told the homeowner I would be happy to help, setting aside my internal anxiety at the ability to perform the scope of work.

I got an estimate written up, materials scheduled for delivery, and a commercial-sized lift was on site the day we were scheduled to start. It was daunting. As soon as Kevin and I began the tear-off, underneath the metal-wrapped fascia and the vented sheets of soffit, were the original 1 x 3 soffit boards and fascia. There was an enormous problem: everything was lead painted. Okay, now the job is eons out of my scope. I approached the homeowner and let them know our findings. The homeowner, immediately looking defeated, shared his concern with me; he was worried this would be the case.

He said, "I understand if you can't do the work. I will happily pay you for your service so far and we will figure something out."

Immediately, I told him, "Let me get certified in lead-safe renovation and I will do the job. We are here. I can do it."

Overwhelmed with joy, the homeowner was happy to allow us to step off the job and get the required training.

I turned to Kevin, and I said, "We do lead work now."

We both took the class, and off we go heading back to the monstrosity of a project that even large, seasoned construction companies wanted nothing to do with. As we tear everything out and ensure the site is always tarped and clean, I learn that hundred-year-old framework on a monster house is never an ideal situation. We had to block out and reframe that entire roof rim as well as all three peak structures. A task I had never done, especially so high up, but again, we're here, so let's get it done.

I was blocking out the front peak of the house, the most prominent peak on the home. At the tip of the peak, you're close to forty feet in the air. Strapped to my lift, my frame gun in one hand and a 2 x 4 in the other, I tack in my blocking. I reach over the top to level the board out. Once it is exactly where I want it, I send another frame nail through it. But I shot the frame nail right through my right pointer finger. Oh man, thinking about that even today still makes me cringe. The second problem I had tacked my blocking in, so I stuck to the tip of a forty-foot peak. In an adrenaline-rushed rant, I grabbed my circular saw, and dangerously cut the board out so I could get back to the ground. Once I got to the ground, Kevin looked at me: I am ghost white. I removed the board from the nail, and now I just have the nail to deal with. But it went through the bone and my adrenaline is wearing thin. Any effort I attempt to pull it through on my own fails. I have no choice but to go to the emergency room. Luckily, I am still on my Tri-Care Health insurance.

I get to the hospital. After X-rays, removal, and a good cleaning, I am bandaged up and sent on my way. I head back to the job site to finish out the day's work. The homeowners are floored that I am even on their property, but grateful their job is continuing. The lesson I am sharing here is, when you're committed, there is not much in this world that can stop you, and commitment runs deep within me.

Our first home build ever was in the state of Missouri. I remember I told my wife, "If I can build a home in another state, I can build a home anywhere in Iowa." And we did. We built a house outside of Kirksville and it was beautiful. From a location, logistical, and manpower standpoint, it was hard, but I did it. It was yet another referral and the homeowners couldn't find a contractor to work on their lake house. I would later learn the locals refer to "Spring Lake" as "Devils Lake."

The job was complicated enough, but being in another state was challenging. I delivered materials with my flatbed because our local supplier wouldn't deliver over state lines, not to mention on-site. If you needed to make a material run at the local Menards or Home Depot, you were gone for the greater part of two hours. It was a disaster as we were walking through it, but we persevered. The day the homeowners and I did our final walk-through, the smiles on their faces and the fact they could enjoy their home certainly made me happy. I learned a lot from that project. We all did. And we carry those lessons into every job we do.

I have learned throughout my brief career as a business owner that when you focus on the people, the people will always take care of you. As a company, we have always had a mentality of "There is no job too small." Most would argue that my mind expands to the other end of the bell curve: "There is no job too large." This is very true, especially for my waterproofing company.

I had an email sent to me once from a general contractor that said, "I know this scope is outside of your current capabilities, but I wanted to send it to you, so you knew what we're doing and what we are looking for."

I simply responded with, "Nothing is over my capabilities."

CHAPTER 18

WE ARE CARPENTERS, ASPIRING TO BE ARTISTS

I HAVE LEARNED THROUGHOUT MY CAREER THAT construction is an art form. I tell my clients, "We are carpenters, aspiring to be artists."

I would like to introduce the client, Jennie B. Jennie's job started out small and simple. She lives in Grinnell, where HR is prominent. Around June 2022, I receive an email from her requesting I come and look at her front porch. She mentioned she had heard great things about my company, not to mention her house was just a stone's throw away from the job we were currently working on.

Upon my first arrival to Jennie's house, I realize her house is the "old pink house." I remember from high school all the older people in town would mention that it was a hardware store downtown and later moved to her property. Jennie and I meet, and we walk through the front porch together. She describes her wants and desires for her front porch and I get to work writing up a bid to present to her. She accepted the scope of work at the agreed-upon price and we get to work.

An unfortunate turn of events comes shortly after we begin working on Jennie's home: her mother passes away and Jennie makes memorial service arrangements while mourning the loss of her mother. My staff and I were quick to share our support and if there was anything she needed, to the best of our ability, we would make it happen. Once Jennie is finished with her family situation, she approaches me about potentially doing a kitchen remodel. We are sitting out on a small patio discussing the remodel. Jennie is going this way and that way, possibly taking down this wall, putting up another wall, and making an addition on the back, and putting on new siding.

By this time, I muster up the question and say, "Jennie, what's your budget here?"

She says, "Well, I don't really have one."

"Well, Jennie, there must be a budget. What you're talking about doing will get expensive real fast."

We agree to do the addition. We will also replace the siding, since it was pink asbestos tile siding. As we start work, we recognize immediately that the basement is in no shape whatsoever to be sound enough to attach the foundation for the addition. I ask the Director of Buildings and Permits over for an inspection before we get too far. He shows up and immediately shuts the job down. In a panic, I mustered every International Building Code stored in the vault of my mind to plead a case of how we could do it. To no avail. (Don't judge me. It was worth a shot and every contractor has done it at some point.) I have to call Jennie and have a hard conversation with her. Something I would find that we would have a lot of.

Jennie says, "Well, how much would a new basement cost?"

Oh gosh, never have I lifted a house in the air and ripped out the old basement to put a new one in. I simply reply with, "I don't know, but I can certainly get that information for you." Here comes the second side of every coin you choose to flip. With lifting the house and how old it was (her house was built in 1865), there were serious concerns about literally everything: the walls, the joists, the roof. Everything was a concern because I could foresee lifting this home and it would crumble.

I worked with Jennie to help find a company that can come in and replace the foundation. I request to be contracted with the company I want in place of the one she does because, although it is her house, it is my job site. I wanted everything to flow through me or my general manager. That way we could ensure things were in order and we could limit the telephone game. I learned a long time ago, never put the homeowner in the middle of your project except to decide on materials. We found a basement company and we get on their schedule.

Luckily, when Jennie's mom passed away, she and her sister inherited her apartment across town. So, she was unaffected by the worst side of construction projects, which is living in them. Meanwhile, Jennie begins to daydream about her home and the beauty it once had. It really came about when we were replacing the siding. Under the pink asbestos tile siding was the original redwood siding, painted yellow in the 1800s. After inspecting it, we learned quickly there was no way to save it: it had to come off. As we are pulling off the east wall, we find a surprise. There is a circus advertisement that spans the whole side of the house from a circus in 1866. The advertisement was badly battered from years of ambient air and moisture infiltration. And as soon as we removed the siding, it began to disintegrate.

Jennie, a professional music historian, finds herself overjoyed. The fact that her house was once a hardware store downtown convinced her to respect and preserve and protect this structure. There is one problem with that. When a house is so old, and has been neglected for so long, it gets to a point where there isn't much left to preserve. It is an unfortunate truth, but if you're in the restoration business, then you will understand. Now, Jennie and I discuss restoring her entire home to time-period-specific matchings. I am talking corbels, dentil molding, custom crown atop the windows and doors, custom interior trim, doors, rosettes, plinth blocks. The level of craftsmanship on this job is at a level that most carpenters wouldn't touch in their lifetime. I don't say that to be disrespectful to any carpenter out there. It's that this job was immense and risky; very few carpenters would take it on. It will require me as the business owner to step into a better version of myself. Lucky for Jennie, that was what I needed at that moment.

Now, here came the second portion of the job: how the hell do I bid this thing out? This home isn't a spec home where you slap it together from a plan set and everything is marginalized to the penny within the budget. This is a custom home on steroids. This is a home where you don't know what you don't know. I did my due diligence in the beginning: I proposed we could knock it down and rebuild it for a fraction of the cost. That was an absolute hard no from Jennie.

I presented Jennie with three options. I referred to it as the Used Toyota, the Cadillac, and the Rolls Royce. Jennie was delighted and of course, she insisted on the Rolls Royce package. Jennie signed the contract with more confidence than John Hancock had when he signed the Declaration of Independence; she used a calligraphy pen as well. After many shopping days, design meetings, and daydreaming from us both, we have a solid plan. Bring this house back to life: make it big, make it beautiful, make it crazy. And all those things we did.

People don't understand how hard it is to own and operate a business. HR was my third attempt at a business (my second was yet another shot in the dark that never went anywhere. Not only that, I was so consumed with fear of what happened the last time that I never took it fully off the ground), and it makes me remember never to stop giving up on what you feel you're meant to do and who you're meant to be. When Jennie put her faith in me with her home, I made it my mission to ensure that every single day, she knew she had made the right choice. I became so interested in her house that I found myself at the county courthouse for days, searching through old title records tracing the history of her home. It was an expanding experience for me. We affirmed things we already knew and learned a few new pieces of information that helped us key in the original owner and builder of her home.

You would think only Tom Silva of *This Old House* was qualified to embark on what we did. No explanation that I could ever write on paper would ever do it justice. So instead, here is a photo for you to review.

The corbels were made in our wood shop with our CNC router. The dentil molding, frost boards, front door frame, crown molding, outside corners, rosettes, plinth blocks were either made on-site, or in our wood shop. We had custom copper drip edge made, custom half-round copper gutters, leader heads, and downspouts. Human hands touched every square inch of this home. My mom even designed and built the stained glass above the door. Nothing on or in this house was mass manufactured. Jennie B and her home deserved to bring a level of craftsmanship back to life, in a world where mass manufacturing just makes too much sense.

Jennie's house became the talk of the town, newspapers, and a TV show. Everyone was interested to know what was going on with the "old pink house." When Brent Roske, (the owner of the Flamingo Network) approached us about filming the home and letting the world know what we were doing, I made it explicitly clear that this is Jennie's home and it's her story. He made a TV show called *Spruce It Up* on the Flamingo Network on Roku.

Sadly, in June 2023, Jennie was diagnosed with ALS and given less than two years to live. I will never forget that day she texted me and the meeting that followed. The person who had become family to me, believed in me more and treated me better than any of my own family ever did, was about to leave me. We both cried at her dining room table.

I looked at Jennie and I said, "Jennie, it isn't about how long we live, it's about how we live." And I was committed to ensuring that Jennie B lived the most fulfilling rest of her life as I could possibly give her.

It became, "What memories can we make?" Shortly after Jennie's diagnosis, we formed a team within HR to band together and attend the Walk to Defeat ALS. Jennie designed our team shirts (with medieval musical script) and was the guest of honor as we all walked beside her. We all hung keys together on the ALS board. (ALS's theme is the Key to unlock ALS.)

Jennie B and her project have inspired me in more ways than I could have ever thought possible. Jennie not only became a very important client whom everyone in HR holds near to themselves, but she became a friend to me, my family, and everyone in HR. She became a person to look up to, to look forward to meeting, and to always remember when the time comes that we are no longer able to perform work for her. What started out as just a simple front porch turned into a beautiful home and a beautiful friendship. Thank you, Jennie B. You are truly an inspiration. HR will always be Team Jennie B., and I promise, every single year, I will hang a key for you, Jennie.

CHAPTER 19

THE END OF THE STORY

SO, YOU MAY BE ASKING, WELL, HOW DID IT ALL END? Believe it or not, I went back to DMACC in the Spring Semester 2020. Right, wrong, or indifferent, I wanted to finish what I started many years ago. I graduated from DMACC in December 2020 as an honor student. Today, that diploma hangs proudly in my office at HomeRevisions. DMACC and I settled our dispute on October 12, 2020. What had been a pursuit to find the truth for so long would come about, and I found my own truth through the whole journey: I am capable, I am willing, and there is nothing that will ever stop me from achieving what and who I am supposed to become. It showed me we are truly in charge of our own destinies, no matter how hard life kicks you in the face.

The day before I settled, I set up a meeting with Ean at DMACC. I explained everything to him, saying, "I believe this account was fake. Everything you guys have done was to cover your ass." I then stood up, looking him in the eyes, with my hand held out confidently, saying the three most powerful words any of us can ever speak: "I forgive you." I shook his hand and left. That is what my own chaos throughout my life had taught me. Always choose forgiveness, because at the end of the day, there comes a point where the weight is no longer yours to carry. So let it go and start living your life.

Since graduating from DMACC, I completed a course with Goldman Sachs (10,000 Small Businesses). Most recently, I have completed Harvard Business School Online, where I studied Leadership. Taylor and I live a happy, quiet life, surrounded by people we love. I am thankful to have her and our family to come home to every single night; they are and will always be my greatest reason "why."

My father sees me now, and I see him. We both have put a lot of work into being better for ourselves, so we can be better for each other. The relationship I have with him today is the relationship that, growing up, I always craved. My father is a great man and a role model for me. My father has grown to become one of my best friends, and I get just as excited as I did when I was a little boy when I see his number show up on my phone. The man who was harder to get ahold of than the Secretary of Defense is now someone who makes sure he answers or calls back in no time at all. That's power. My father found the love of his life, Kristy, and I was honored to stand next to him as they got married. She is a beautiful soul and the perfect person for my dad.

My mother and I have rebuilt our relationship as well. About a year ago, I sat her down, and I took responsibility for my part in the chaos of my upbringing. I apologized for leaving at such a young age, and in the way that I did. Now I see the love she has for me, my wife, and our daughter. A mother's love is something you can never truly understand. I know I got my craftsmanship ability from my mother's side of the family. Today, I encouraged my mom to start her own company, and she did. Any chance I can, I give her jobs here and there so she can live her artistic dreams (like the stained glass on Jennie B's house). That is how my mother and I have grown. I am proud of her, and I know she is proud of me.

My stepdad and I have rekindled in ways I never knew could be possible. I know he carries a heavy burden of everything that happened. Every time we spoke, all he could say was, "I wish all you kids were young again. I would do everything differently." Finally, I told him, "I hope you know I hold nothing against you. It is because of you and the things that happened that I am the man I am today." I would never want to go back and do that over because I love the man I am today. I wouldn't be this man if my life had played out any other way.

I choose to love my parents and my stepdad, and I choose to make sure they are a continuous part of my life. That is what forgiveness bears: the option of choice. You can forgive, but you can never forget. Are these memories your power or are they your chaos? All of us siblings have grown and are walking our own paths. I like to say, "We all dealt with our upbringing in our own way." That's okay, that's the point of everything. Deal with things the best way we know how. But do everything you can to pursue a path of a greater you.

Finally, the Iowa National Guard, I proudly served. Very proudly. There was nothing more fulfilling than going to drill on the weekends and working with my lower enlisted to be a guide for them. Going from the once-struggling junior enlisted who couldn't make it to drill because he didn't have gas money to showing up ready every month with a coach's mentality.

Many of us in the army serve for the same purpose and share similar struggles. It's very fulfilling for me to see those young soldiers, and I can sense immediately if they are going through some shit. I am always there for them, standing in front of them to remind them they are not their past. The decision is theirs to "Be all that you can be." There is no greater feeling on this earth than to watch these young men and women find their power and project it out into the world. Keep it up, troops. I am always eager to watch you grow, and I will never be too busy for you to think you can't call upon me at any time.

The life I have endured won for me the power to overcome anything in front of me. It takes grit; it takes a willingness to step into a better version of you, and it takes passion—passion for people and passion for yourself and who you're becoming, passion for what you're doing, and a passion for the impact you're making through your company. If you can zero in on those key things, I promise you will be successful in whoever you venture to become.

The most important thing I hope you take from my story is that you can't take it all on alone. The Nick Darland that writes to you today, would not be that person without the people mentioned in this book. And yes, I do mean even those that hurt me along the way. I am worth it, more importantly, you are worth it. Nothing is a detour; it is all a part of the journey. However, stepping into the unknown will require a new version of yourself that does not yet exist. That next version of you is what life expects, if you ever wish to live a life that is better than what you have now. The things that happen, happen for us, not to us. Taking your power and projecting it into the world in a productive, positive manner is your responsibility, just as it is mine. Have faith in everything you do, because without faith, what are we?

You are capable beyond measure, and you can do anything you set your mind to. Where you put your blame is where you put your power. Everything starts and ends with you. So, do the things that are necessary for you. Take that pen and write your own story. Make it big, make it beautiful, and make it crazy, because you only live one life. So go all out, always. Thank you for walking along this journey with me. It has been a vulnerable, emotional, and, most importantly, releasing experience for me. I am truly thankful.

As I wrap up my story, I am taken back to the night I left my mom's and the voice in my head saying, "Stay where you are, and you will become everything that people have always expected you to be." I am reminded of the vision, of a life without trauma. Here's the funny thing I have realized—the trauma will always be a part of me, but it will never define me, and hardships, well as you grow, the hardships will grow. You just find yourself in a state of being able to handle the weight a whole lot better.

My story encompasses just the first twenty-eight years of my life. I fully understand that I haven't even scratched the surface of who I am supposed to be. I say to myself (and others) frequently, "Nick, this is you at twenty-eight. Just imagine yourself at thirty-eight, forty-eight, fifty-eight, etc." That person is someone I look forward to meeting when the time comes. Until then, I will continue to do more, be more, and become more.

ACKNOWLEDGMENTS

Jeff:

Your presence in my life has been a beacon of light during my darkest moments. Your guidance and our conversations have been invaluable as I navigate through the chaos. Thank you for showing me how to transform adversity into productive growth.

Chaplain Craig:

Thank you for being my rock when I had nowhere else to turn. Your simple act of listening showed me the power of compassion and empathy.

Matt:

Your belief in me and your willingness to take a chance on the unknown have been instrumental in my journey. Your words, "It's time to start that next chapter," echo in my mind as I conclude this book.

Jennie B:

Your friendship has been a source of inspiration and strength. Without your unwavering belief in me, this book would never have come to fruition. From the depths of my heart, thank you for your kindness and constant support.

John and Traci:

Your family would be the first of many to show me the way toward being a light. It is something you never had to do, but the fact you did mended my life. Traci, Jon, Natalie, and Matthew: I now see the sacrifice you all as a family made for me. You took me in as a broken kid who was full of struggle, confusion, and chaos, and you loved me as if I were one of your own. Whether you realize it or not, you are the reason I am who I am today. I honor the fact that you took me in; it has developed my heart in service to others. Your family will always be a key part in my testimony. From the bottom of my heart. Thank you.

Jon and Kerry:

Your generosity and support during a time of need have touched my heart deeply. I look back on my time spent with you, and I am so thankful. You took me in when I had nowhere to go and provided a home for me for two years—never once asking for anything in return. You truly gave me hope for a brighter future during a time when it was hard to see the next day ahead of me. Thank you.

Larry and Lil:

From my earliest days, you have been a guiding light in my life. Your support and love have meant more to me than words can express. Thank you.

Ron and Sherry:

Your generosity and support when I started HomeRevisions eased the burden of self-employment. I will always cherish the gift of Ol' Blue and the role you played in my journey.

Stephanie and Bruce:

Your unwavering support for Taylor and me is a constant source of strength and inspiration. Your belief in us ignites our dreams, both personally and professionally. Thank you for always being there for us.

Kelly and Karma:

Thank you for being my second family. What began as a simple friendship between two young kids has blossomed into a lifelong bond, and I am profoundly grateful I get to share my passionate pursuit with Kolton and Kevin every single day. I love you all.

Mom and Dad:

You did the best you could with what you had, and I promise to ensure that your efforts never go unnoticed. I am deeply grateful to each of you. Because of you, I will do more, be more, and become more. I love you both.

Taylor:

Your love and support have been my rock. I tell you frequently that you are the strongest person I have ever met. Your commitment to me and my life pushes me on the days I don't feel I can measure up. I am forever grateful for that first date—February 17, 2019, was the day I knew I had met my forever person. You and our family will always be my deepest reason why. I love you.

Andi Grace:

You are my reason for everything. From the moment you were born, you have filled my heart with pure joy, and I am committed to giving you the best life possible. Every day I watch you get bigger and more beautiful. You are so smart and so much like your mother, I am so lucky and grateful to be your father. You inspire me to leap into the unknown and be the man you can look up to. I love you more than you'll ever know, little girl.

Faithlyn Rose:

There isn't a single day that your mother and I don't think about you and wonder what kind of beautiful girl you would have been—the impact you would have had on this world and the lives you would have changed. It is those ideas that push me every single day to ensure that you have your chance at life, even though you aren't physically with us. Your mother and I love you so much.

Michael Mcpherren:

In memory of Michael Mcpherren, your friendship was a beacon of light during my darkest days. Your wisdom and support helped me find the courage to make difficult decisions for a brighter future. Though I miss you dearly every day, I will never forget the impact you had on my life. Rest in peace, my friend.

Jeff Vander Beek:

In memory of Jeff Vander Beek, your friendship was a formidable guide in my life. During times of darkness, we found solace in each other's company, sharing hopes and dreams for a better tomorrow. Our conversations still echo in my mind, a testament to the bond we shared. Rest in peace, my friend.

My stepdad:

Thank you for being there during a time when my own father couldn't be. Regardless of right, wrong, or indifferent concerning the things that happened as we were growing up, I love you and I forgive you.

DMACC:

Thank you for the experience. Right or wrong, I finished what I started, and you allowed me to do so. The circumstances and events that happened between us, I would never ask to take back and do over. It was the teetering point in my life and for that, I will always be grateful.

Mrs. Wolfe:

Thank you for being such a huge support in my life, even to this day. You have cheered me on in the background since my senior year; please know, it has never gone unnoticed. Thank you.

Mrs. Allen:

From the once struggling kid who was always on probation, sitting in fear in your office to the man who mustered up the courage to share his story with the world. Your kindness and belief taught me so many lessons that I now truly understand. Thank you.

www.ingramcontent.com/pod-product-compliance
Lightning Source LLC
Chambersburg PA
CBHW070144080526
44586CB00015B/1839